James Jones was Bishop of Hull from 1994 to 1998, then Bishop of Liverpool from 1998 to 2013. From 2010 to 2018, he chaired three independent panels – the Hillsborough Independent Panel, the Independent Panel on Forestry and the Gosport Independent Panel. In 2016, he was granted the Freedom of the City of Liverpool and appointed a KBE for services to justice and the bereaved. He has been a regular contributor to BBC Radio 4's 'Thought for the Day' on the *Today* programme. He and Sarah have three daughters – Harriet, Jemima and Tabitha – and two grandchildren, Ben and Sophie.

JUSTICE FOR CHRIST'S SAKE

A personal journey around justice
through the eyes of faith

James Jones

First published in Great Britain in 2021

Society for Promoting Christian Knowledge
36 Causton Street
London SW1P 4ST
www.spck.org.uk

British Library Cataloguing-in-Publication Data
A catalogue record for this book is available from the British Library

ISBN 978–0–281–08625–2
eBook ISBN 978–0–281–08626–9

1 3 5 7 9 10 8 6 4 2

Typeset by Manila Typesetting Company
First printed in Great Britain by Ashford Colour Press

eBook by Manila Typesetting Company

Produced on paper from sustainable forests

For
Ben and Sophie

There is always one moment in childhood when the door
opens and lets the future in.
(Graham Greene, *The Power and the Glory*)

Jesus was angry and said, 'Let the children come to me . . . the
Kingdom of God is theirs'.
(Luke 14, my translation)

Contents

Plates

A picture of my consecration in 1994, painted by our daughter, Harriet

Ben, five, and Sophie, three – our grandchildren

Hillsborough Independent Panel in the Lady Chapel, Liverpool Cathedral, 12 September 2012

Margaret Aspinall, Chair of the Hillsborough Family Support Group, addressing the second inquest, 11 May 2016

Anne Williams, founder of Hope for Hillsborough, attending the Hillsborough memorial service, 15 April 2013, shortly before her death

A gift from the Cathedral Chapter of the poem 'Liverpool', about Hillsborough, by Carol Ann Duffy and illustrated by Stephen Raw

Montage portrait by Anthony Brown from the '100 Heads Thinking as One' exhibition to mark Liverpool as 'Capital of Culture' in 2008

Ardhentu Chatterjee working with the landless, West Bengal

Nariman Gasimoglu giving his paper on the Amazon

Pastor Joel Hunter and Jim Ball consult with Sir John Houghton on caring for the environment

Tim Parry, killed in the Warrington bombings in 1993 and inspiration of the Tim Parry Johnathan Ball Peace Foundation

Anthony Walker, murdered with an axe, 30 July 2005, aged 18

Dome of the Rock, Jerusalem

Church of the Holy Sepulchre, Jerusalem, with the guardian who offered me the key

Plates

'If you're the Bishop I'm the Pope'. Gift from a prisoner on the occasion of a visit to HM Prison Risley
Icon: 'I am the light of the world'

Now when John had heard in the prison the works of Christ, he sent two of his disciples, and said unto him, Art thou he that should come, or do we look for another? Jesus answered and said unto them, Go and shew John again those things which ye do hear and see:

The blind receive their sight, and the lame walk, the lepers are cleansed, and the deaf hear, the dead are raised up, and the poor have the Gospel preached to them. And blessed is he whosoever shall not be offended in me.

(MATTHEW 11.2—6, BOOK OF COMMON PRAYER)

Preface

One of the first fully formed sentences that a child speaks is, 'That's not fair!' Whether sharing a bag of sweets or taking turns in a game, children are acutely aware of what is their due. Woe betide anyone who shares the sweets unevenly or leaves someone out! They do not need a lesson in philosophy to express or explain their indignation. It's intuitive. Of course, by the time they get to play pass the parcel at a party they may well have been socialized or trained by their parents or carers, but the vehemence with which they shout, 'It's my turn!' suggests such a grasp of the moral order that the other young players are challenged to acknowledge it and to give way. 'That's not fair' is an appeal to something greater. You could argue that by playing the game the children have simply entered into a contract with each other. But when the rules are broken it's more than the contract that is breached. A greater rule has been violated. It is about being fair and acting fairly. This is the principle that lies behind the game and gives meaning and purpose to life itself.

Although philosophers and theologians have laboured since the days of Aristotle and Plato to unravel the mysteries of fairness and justice, most of us come to these great issues like children. It is only when something unfair happens to us, or when we encounter a situation which feels unjust, that we engage with the issue of injustice. While academics write books about it, it is those who suffer injustice who are compelled by their wounds to do something about it and are spurred on to right the wrong.

My own journey around justice has not been and is not an academic exercise, but arose out of my calling to be a pastor and – I hope this does not sound too grand – 'to heal the broken-hearted'. It was the aching hearts of the families, particularly the mothers of the babies and children who had died in Alder Hey Hospital in Liverpool, that first alerted me pastorally to a serious injustice when I became Bishop of Liverpool. Without the permission of the families, thousands of organs and tissue samples of their dead children had been retained by the hospital without their consent or their knowledge. And then it was the broken hearts of the bereaved and of the survivors of the Hillsborough Stadium disaster in 1989 that set me on the path of seeing the world through the eyes of victims of injustice as they struggled to be heard in their search for truth and justice over the deaths of their 96 loved ones.

But the word 'justice' (and, perhaps even more, 'injustice') covers a multitude of meanings. There is 'justice' as an act of judgement. This is where something has gone wrong or someone has done wrong and demanding justice is about holding the guilty to account. This is the theme of the Hillsborough narrative in Chapter 1, where the demand for justice is about getting to the truth in order to find out how and why the 96 died, and then holding those responsible to account.

Then there is 'justice' as a description of a state of affairs in which the relationships between different persons and parties are deemed to be harmonious, where everybody receives what is their due and where there is reciprocal respect and honour. This is the justice by which we measure the moral depth and breadth of a society. This expression of justice will be seen in the chapters on the city, the Earth and race.

And then there is 'justice' as a virtue that is found in people who are conscience-bound and morally disposed to render to each person his or her due. It describes the character of an individual motivated to do what is right by and for other people. From the pages of our history, one such example would be William Wilberforce, who features in Chapter 2. In his day, such a just person would have been called 'righteous'.

When it comes to defining what is just, most of us would follow the thinking of the philosopher John Rawls, who saw justice as forming a triad of freedom, equality and opportunity – freedom to be and to act as freely as possible without infringing on the liberty of others; equal before the law in all things; and having the opportunity to access socially and economically whatever one's talents would allow one to achieve. A just society would rely not simply on the virtues of its citizens but also on the structures it puts in place to protect them from the vices of its members.

Judging what is just when it comes to our actions causes us to consider three aspects: the intention or the motive, the nature of the act itself, and its consequences. Weighing up each of these will guide us in knowing what makes for a more just world.

In our day, we are witnessing social upheaval on a seismic scale as we respond to the COVID-19 pandemic. A shift in values is already underway. The media have highlighted the deep diversity of the UK, celebrated peace-time heroism, brought to the fore the role of science in public policy and focused on the culture of ageing and dying with an urgency not hitherto seen.

Over the decades, the voting pattern of the British people has been to swing between the two polarities of self-improvement and social fairness. There now seems to be a more acute awareness that the lower-paid are unfairly bearing the brunt of the pandemic: care workers, nurses, those isolating in poor accommodation, those on zero-hour contracts and some of our minority ethnic communities. There's also a sharper focus on the elderly and other vulnerable groups, such as the lonely, the homeless and the mentally ill. The legacy of this crisis could well result in the emergence of a stronger public mood to address historic imbalances, while at the same time seeking to restore the economy. Embracing both polarities may defy previous voting prejudices as the old nostrums fail to inspire.

At the same time, there has been widespread expectation of and support for government intervention. The question for the future will be which areas of national life should take priority in a future programme of interventionism. Health? The elderly? The environment? Education? The economy? International development? Packed into that little word 'should' is the notion of fairness, as well as what is practical and pragmatic.

If the disadvantaged become more deprived and if advancing technology leads to greater unemployment, what are the moral and economic arguments to be advanced for and against a universal basic income? Will future pay levels match the new-found worth of our key and front-line workers? In the complementary needs of the old and the young, might we see a strengthening of family bonds? The elderly need to be reconnected with the younger generation to assist in their care and the young need support from the previous generation with both finance and housing. Might the taxation system see a radical realignment to reinforce the mutual responsibility of the generations for each other? With the need to raise greater funds to pay for our social needs, might we see an increase in taxation with a particular focus on raw materials? In turn, might this lead to less consumption at a time when we realize that the Earth is not a limitless larder and its capacity to produce food is under threat from both overpopulation and the changing climate?

These are some of the questions that have more of an edge in a post-pandemic world. However we try to answer them, the question that will never disappear, like an air bubble in a badly hung roll of wallpaper, is 'What is fair?' In early 2021, Amol Rajan presented a series on BBC Radio 4 called 'Rethink Fairness'. It was a response, he said, to a consensus among the radio audience that there should be greater fairness in our post-pandemic world.

Even though experts proposed different solutions, there was unanimity about the ethical imperative to be fair. No one seemed to dispute this certainty. Should anyone think that we live in a morally relativistic age, 'fairness' is emerging as the new moral absolute. The theme was taken up by Mark Carney, previously Governor of the Bank of England, in his 2020 Reith Lectures. In his third lecture, 'From Covid crisis to Renaissance', he acknowledged how the pandemic had revealed deep strains in our society. He argued that 'we need to act as an interdependent community' and pleaded that 'the values of economic dynamism and efficiency have been joined by those of solidarity, fairness, responsibility and compassion'. Without doubt, there has been a turning up of the volume of the voice calling for a world that is more just. Furthermore, discussions about fairness and justice are not just theoretical but for many are also now a matter of life and death.

The chapters that follow are limited to and by the furrow that I have ploughed in my own journey concerning justice. I frequently turn to the example of Jesus. Those things that I have thought, said and done intuitively have gained an authority for me when I have found that they are in keeping with the sayings and actions of Jesus about acting justly, loving mercy and walking humbly with God. For those looking for encouragement to follow their moral intuition, even to swim against the tide, and to be fair in all their dealings, I hope that this little book will reinforce their resolve.

I have written this book during the months of lockdown. The periods of isolation have magnified the issues that it addresses. During the past year our little grandson Ben has been in therapy following the removal of a brain tumour as he turned six years old. The unfairness of the suffering of an innocent child has never been far from my thoughts and has added another dimension to how unfair the world sometimes seems. At times it has sapped any enthusiasm for writing.

Preface

The way in which Ben and Sophie, his sister, two years younger, are living their young lives in the light of all that they have endured has filled us, their family, with awe and delight. I humbly dedicate this book to them in the hope that a fairer world awaits.

Advent 2020

Acknowledgements

On my journey around justice, Sarah my wife has been my companion, as have our three daughters, Harriet, Jemima and Tabitha. Sarah was one of the original team that set up the charity Tearfund. She has an intuitive wisdom about people and situations. Whereas I take time to form a view, she sees quickly and is invariably right. During our fifteen years in Liverpool, we shared our home with colleagues who are now our friends – Margaret, who helped me with this book, as well as Phil, Edwina, Sandra, Wendy, Tom, Christine, Debbie, Dennis and Robin. Each knows the debt we will always owe them. Bishops David and Richard, successive Bishops of Warrington, with huge generosity helped make this journey possible.

I am grateful to the Revd Linda Bloom and to the students of both the Harrogate School of Theology & Mission and the St Hilda Easter School, who encouraged me to put pen to paper and write about justice from a Christian perspective.

I acknowledge with special thanks permission granted to reproduce extracts from the following in this book. (I also acknowledge where permission has been sought but is awaited at the time of printing.)

BBC Radio 4, 'Thought for the Day', *Today* programme. The copyright in the transcripts is the property of the BBC and is used under licence (copyright © BBC).

John Buchan (1941) *Sick Heart River* (London: Hodder & Stoughton). Copyright © the Lord Tweedsmuir and Jean,

Lady Tweedsmuir. Reproduced by permission of the Licensor through PLS Clear.

Nick Cave (1997) 'Into my arms'. Permission sought.

Kenneth Clark (1986) *The Other Half: A self-portrait* (London: Hamish Hamilton). Permission sought.

Nariman Gasimoglu (2010) 'Spiritual reading guide on shared nature: Commonalities in Bible and Koran from eco-theology perspectives', *Journal of Azerbaijani Studies* (13, pp. 3–4). Reproduced by kind permission of the author.

William Hague (2007) *William Wilberforce: The life of the great anti-slave trade campaigner* (London: HarperCollins). Reproduced by permission of HarperCollins Publishers. Copyright © 2007 William Hague.

Michael Jackson (1991) 'Heal the world'. Permission sought.

Lord Igor Judge (2015) *The Safest Shield* (Oxford: Hart Publishing). Reproduced by permission of Hart Publishing, Bloomsbury Publishing Plc. Copyright © Lord Igor Judge.

Simon Sebastian Montefiore (2011) *Jerusalem* (London: Weidenfeld & Nicholson). Reproduced by permission of Weidenfeld and Nicholson, Orion Publishing Group. Copyright © Simon Sebag Montefiore.

Colin and Wendy Parry (1995) *Tim: An ordinary boy* (London: Hodder & Stoughton). Reproduced by permission of Hodder & Stoughton.

Jonathon Porritt (2020) *Hope in Hell: A decade to confront the climate emergency* (London: Simon & Schuster). Reproduced by kind permission of the author.

The Shawshank Redemption (Warner Brothers, 1994), story by Stephen King. Reproduced by permission of Warner Brothers. Permission sought from Stephen King.

R. S. Thomas, 'The prisoner'. Copyright © Elodie Thomas; reproduced by kind permission.

1

Hillsborough

I always hesitate to talk or to write about Hillsborough. It feels to me as if the only ones who have the right and the authority to speak about the tragedy are those who lost their loved ones or those who survived the disaster. Although I am among those whose lives have been affected by the trauma of it, nothing in our experience compares with the suffering of the bereaved and the survivors. When, on certain occasions, I have thought it right to speak out, I know there are a few who object to my voice being heard. I know too that by putting pen to paper I risk further alienating them, so I have to be very clear, at least to myself, as to why I am doing this.

As far as I am able to judge, chairing the Hillsborough Independent Panel was the single most important aspect of my work as Bishop of Liverpool from 1998 to 2013. It brought into the sharpest focus, for me, issues that all of us struggle with – the problem of suffering, the pain of loss, living with grief, the corruption of power and the lack of justice in the world. These and other sad life events are made all the more difficult to bear by trying to square them with a belief in God, who seems to have neither the will nor the power to intervene.

In giving an account of my involvement in the Hillsborough narrative, I am offering an account of myself as a Christian pastor trying to marry this tragic story to my allegiance to Jesus Christ and his own experience of injustice on this earth. But I offer it also to the families of the 96 and the survivors of Hillsborough, even knowing that some, for very good reasons, will reject it as irrelevant to their continuing grief and anger. And I offer it to the wider public as the testimony of one human being to another about living in a manifestly unjust world.

There's a saying from one of the psalms:

Thou desirest truth in the inward being
Therefore teach me wisdom in my secret heart.
(Psalm 51, Book of Common Prayer)

In these pages, I bare my soul in pursuit of wisdom. It was the families and survivors of Hillsborough who impressed on my inner being the burning imperatives of truth and justice. To change the metaphor, truth is a double-edged sword that cuts inwards as well as outwards. While the families fought publicly for the truth for more than thirty years, rising up and challenging the patronizing disposition of unaccountable power of so many institutions, I found myself for ten of those years going deeper into myself, questioning my own ideas and values, as well as my own involvement in a society that had denied for so long both truth and justice to the families of the 96 victims of the Hillsborough disaster.

Justice first and foremost requires the truth to be established. It is not sufficient for that truth to be known only to those who were there and who suffered. The truth of those tragic events needs to be known generally and to be acknowledged by others to be true. It is regrettable that in our relativistic culture we hear people talking about 'my truth' or 'their truth' as if it were impossible to be definite and objective about an event. Justice challenges such subjectivism and relativism. It is predicated on discerning and discovering the truth of what actually happened. That is why getting to the truth of what took place at Hillsborough is so essential for the families. It is not just 'their truth'. The families need to be assured that the nation knows

2

that those who died were 'unlawfully killed', that many could have been saved and that the families were let down by the authorities they trusted. This is the truth that they have needed to hear publicly acknowledged. It is the truth that was obscured for decades, and its denial frustrated the grieving families. It is the truth that was finally recognized when the jury returned a determination of 'unlawfully killed' at the second inquest in 2016, twenty-six years after the tragedy. Without the truth there can be no justice. Yet, conversely, establishing the truth does not guarantee justice and accountability, as the families have gone on to discover.

Although the determination of the second inquest was that the 96 had been 'unlawfully killed', only one person has been convicted, with a fine of £6,500 for a breach of health and safety regulations. For there to be justice, there must also be accountability. Those responsible for wrongdoing should be held accountable. As one mother said to me after the second inquest, 'Now that we know our children were unlawfully killed, we need to know who was responsible.' There is a moral logic to this maternal instinct.

I came to Liverpool in 1998. I had just read Blake Morrison's *As If* (Granta, 2011), his account of the trial of Robert Thompson and Jon Venables, the children who had murdered the child James Bulger in Bootle. It gave me the feeling of coming to a people acquainted with grief. Shortly after my arrival, Trevor and Jenni Hicks, who had lost their two daughters, Sarah and Victoria, came to see me to ask me to preside at the tenth anniversary memorial service of the Hillsborough disaster, an event that took place every year in the football stadium at Anfield in Liverpool. They began to tell me about some of the many unresolved issues relating to the tragedy and its aftermath. These were news to me. Significantly, they had not featured in the Church's briefing for my appointment.

As I listened to Trevor and Jenni, immediately I could see two things. First, the questions they were pursuing appeared reasonable and legitimate; second, they were describing a wound, deep and wide, that had yet to heal. It was the wound not just of a grieving mother and father but also of a whole community that stretched the length and the breadth of the global allegiance to the Liverpool Football Club. Liverpool, as a city, felt the pain, but nearly half of the 96 who died were fans from other parts of the country. The anniversary remembrances bathed the wound year on year, but there was no balm to heal it, for the sore was infected by the lack of truth and accountability for which the families and survivors were campaigning ever more vociferously.

I presided at the tenth, fifteenth and twentieth anniversary services with my Catholic colleague Bishop Tom Williams. These gatherings fell into two parts. The first was a service, with prayers and a gospel choir and the lighting of 96 candles that soothed the grief of the families and the crowd; the second part was like a rally, with rousing speeches demanding that the truth be told about the disaster and those who were responsible should be held to account. The language was strident, the tone vehement and the anger in the crowd palpable. The atmosphere at the twentieth anniversary was tense. More than 30,000 filled the stands. The Prime Minister, Gordon Brown, had recently said that there would never be another enquiry into Hillsborough. That declaration felt like a betrayal.

When Andy Burnham, Secretary of State for Culture, Media and Sport, got up to speak, the crowd was silently hostile. He had begun to wade through a speech he'd taken out of his pocket when the silence was pierced by a lone voice shouting, 'Justice for the 96!' At that sound, the whole stadium rose to its feet to echo the man's cry, and thousands began to chant, 'Justice for the 96!' If you had gathered the crowd into the stadium beforehand to rehearse the sequence, it could not have been more in unison. Sitting alongside Andy Burnham, I felt the force of the voice of the crowd that hemmed us in on all sides. Andy was clearly shaken and, to his credit, returned to London to persuade the Prime Minister to change his mind about Hillsborough.

I am not privy to all the discussions that took place within Government between Number 10, the Home Office and the Ministry of Justice, but a senior civil servant emerged as the pivotal figure who developed the concept of the Hillsborough Independent Panel. Ken Sutton drafted terms of reference that were both politically acceptable to the Government and satisfactory to the majority of the families. They gave the Panel the authority to seek the maximum possible disclosure of all documents relating to the tragedy and its aftermath, to analyse them and to give an account that would add to public understanding.

It was a master-stroke. Ken, with his colleague Ann Ridley, began assembling the Panel, mindful of the expertise needed to act on the terms of reference and in consultation with representatives of the families and survivors so that those appointed by the Home Secretary would have the confidence of those most affected by the tragedy.

Christine Gifford, an expert in freedom of information and data protection, oversaw access to all the material, including the files held by the South Yorkshire Police; Professor Phil Scraton, who had written the definitive account of Hillsborough, oversaw the team of researchers that analysed all the documents; the late Katy Jones, who worked with Jimmy McGovern on the documentary drama about Hillsborough, had personal knowledge of the key figures in the Hillsborough narrative; Paul Leighton, Deputy Chief Constable, guided the members of the Panel in their learning about police documents and procedures; Sarah Tyacke, a former Keeper of Public Records, steered the Panel in creating an archive of all the material; the late Peter Sissons advised the Panel on matters relating to the media, who were themselves implicated in the narrative; Raju Bhatt, a lawyer with vast experience of inquests, guided the Panel in our understanding of the Coronial process.

The Independent Panel was neither an inquiry nor a criminal investigation. It interrogated documents, not people. No one was interviewed under oath. The accessed and analysed documents would tell their own story. The most compelling of these were the post-mortem reports and medical documents analysed by the last member of the Panel, Dr Bill Kirkup. It was this work that eventually persuaded the Attorney General to apply to the High Court to quash the original inquests.

When I was asked to chair the Panel, I sought advice from colleagues and from leaders in the city and the region. Many advised against it as a poisoned chalice. However, those colleagues who would bear the burden of some of the responsibilities that I would have to shed encouraged me to accept, as did Rowan Williams who was then Archbishop of Canterbury. I have to confess that, at this stage, it was not so much the pursuit of truth and justice that persuaded me, but the pastoral needs of the families that I had already met. It was my experience in Hull (to which I will return later) that had begun to impress on me the mission of Jesus to 'heal the broken-hearted'. Even at this point I knew that lives had been shattered by Hillsborough.

Suicides, early deaths, family breakdown, depression and unemployment featured in the lives of the bereaved and the survivors. As a pastor, I felt drawn to them and subconsciously imagined that I would find fulfilment in meeting their need to find answers to their legitimate questions about what had happened to their loved ones and who was responsible.

Alan Johnson, the Home Secretary, announced my appointment as Chair of the Panel. Not all the families were sure that this was the right way to proceed. Some commentators wondered why a bishop had been appointed instead of a judge. In my media interviews I was constantly pressed as to what I expected the outcome to be. Without realizing the full import of my answer, I repeated the terms of reference and replied that 'truth has its own pressure'.

For over twenty years, the families and survivors had felt frustrated and felt let down by the police, the press, politicians, Parliament and by the judiciary itself. Even though, in the past, the Church had been slow to respond to the cries of the families for a thorough inquiry, having been failed by so many institutions, it was to the Church they turned for the chairing of the Panel. Both the Catholic Church and the Church of England, for all their own failings, were known in Liverpool for having the welfare of the people at heart.

Ken and I made a conscious decision that the Panel would meet the families before and on the day of our first meeting as a Panel. We were aware of their distrust and suspicion of those in authority and wanted to assure them that we were not making up our minds before meeting them. We met in the Cunard Building with each of the three family groups separately: the Hillsborough Family Support Group, the Hillsborough Justice Campaign and Hope for Hillsborough. We were already aware of the tensions between the three groups. Peter Sissons, with local roots in the city, expressed surprise at the division. I said that many marriages didn't survive grief, so why should friendships, especially if they had been forged out of grief. It is a feature of many public tragedies that tensions emerge among the bereaved. We resolved to respect and to work with each of the groups. We met first with the largest of the three, the Hillsborough Family Support Group (HFSG), and I began by reading out the names of the 96. This became the glue that bound the Panel together. It tugged tightly at my heart and my calling as a priest and pastor. In the Panel's terms of reference, it was not specified that the Chair should possess any pastoral skills, but from that day on and up until the day we presented our report to the families, and even beyond that day, I found myself drawing deeply on the pastoral skills I had learnt as a priest and a bishop. And not just with the families and survivors but also with the Panel itself.

There were times when the Panel members would feel the full force of the hostility of the families and survivors. We had to understand why, after years of being diminished by those in authority, they were entitled to feel suspicious and to doubt the independence of a body set up by Government. We had to learn to listen through the rage. The anger was also a symptom of grief frustrated and stalled by those in power who sought to protect their own interests.

We set up a Family Liaison subgroup of the Panel that met regularly with the families in a room at Anfield. There were well over a hundred at our first meeting. Just as we were beginning, all the television screens mounted on the walls around the large room came on. The time was precisely 6 minutes past 3 p.m., the time that the match was stopped on 15 April 1989! This was never explained, but the significance did not escape the attention of the families. It felt more than a coincidence. Throughout the period of the Panel's work, there was a team within the Secretariat that remained in constant touch with the families. Often, during the process of public inquiries, victims can feel stranded and alienated by the very procedures that are meant to benefit them by examining the events that led to the tragedy. Maintaining close contact with the families, without becoming biased and thus prejudicing the outcome, was key to keeping their confidence and that of the public.

I felt that we were beginning to make progress when Margaret Aspinall, who became Chair of the HFSG, said to me in front of the families at one of our Liaison meetings: 'This is the first time we've ever been listened to . . . this is the first time that anybody in authority has ever taken us seriously.' Then she added, 'Bishop, you are our last hope'.

Often people would ask me privately and publicly what the families were looking for. Before waiting for any sort of answer, they would suggest that it was 'closure'. From the outset, I refused to use that word, and I continue to eschew it, not least because nobody except the one bereaved has any authority to presume closure for another. Grief is a journey without destination. Moreover, there is no closure to love, nor should there be. In all my conversations with families and survivors, I never once heard anyone talk about closure. Truth, accountability and justice, yes. I began to feel that closure was something that was sought by others who felt discomfited by the relentless, incessant demands for the truth to be told and for those responsible to be held accountable. The notion of closure seemed a useful fiction imagined by those who wished the families would go away.

As I and my colleagues immersed ourselves in accessing and analysing the documents relating to the tragedy and its aftermath, I felt my initial pastoral responses undergo a subtle alchemy, transformed through disbelief and disquiet. When I accepted to chair the Panel, although I was pastorally sympathetic to the unrequited grief of the families, I was genuinely open to what we might find and to what our conclusions might be, but two sets of documents that had an impact on me and my colleagues convinced me that we were in the presence of a scandalous injustice.

Christine Gifford tenaciously pursued the files held by the South Yorkshire Police, Phil Scraton and his team of researchers, assisted by Matt Lewsey from the Secretariat, presented the analysed documents to the Panel to demonstrate conclusively how over 200 police statements written after the tragedy had been altered subsequently to shift the responsibility for the disaster from the police to the fans. The second set of documents was that analysed by Dr Bill Kirkup. They were the post-mortem reports. They showed that the cause of death of the 96 was not as uniform as indicated by the coroner and by the pathologists at the original inquests. In effect, Dr Kirkup was able to advance the convincing theory that forty-one of the 96 might have survived the crush in the pens if the emergency response had been appropriate. I cannot now remember the exact moment when I heard myself uttering these words to the Panel, 'This is the patronizing disposition of unaccountable power', but the more we investigated the documents, the clearer it became that this is what the families had wrestled with for years as they sought answers to their legitimate questions.

My job, as the Chair, was to ensure that the expertise of the different members of the Panel was brought to bear on all the documents. The Panel members were meticulous. We met as a Panel in plenary sessions over thirty times. Two thirds of the way through, I was diagnosed as being in need of a triple heart bypass. I won't repeat here the journey I've described in my book *With My Whole Heart* (SPCK, 2012), but I will record that the first question I asked following the results of my tests was, 'Will I be able to continue with Hillsborough?' I knew we were at a critical stage in the Panel's work. I cannot now recall in detail the answer to my question, but I vividly remember the prayers I made after the operation, pleading with God to help me recover so I could complete the work. It was not lost on me then, nor is it now, that here I was praying to God, who had heard similar cries for help coming from the crowded pens at Hillsborough – cries that were largely unanswered. What right had I to expect God to help me?

As it happened, I had the operation at the end of June 2011 and, with expert care from doctors and nurses and from my wife, and with wonderful support from colleagues, was back working on Hillsborough by the end of August. The Panel's progress during my absence proved all the more how well it worked as a team, which had been chaired in the interim by Peter Sissons.

As we entered the final stretch, it became ever more clear to us from the documents that the families had suffered a series of injustices over the decades. The Panel began to experience something of the antagonism that the families had endured over the years when our work was frustrated, delayed and threatened with judicial review. We sought extra time to deal with the obstacles and to complete our work. Discussion then turned to when and where we should present our report to the families. Right at the outset, we had agreed with the families that they should be the first to read it so that they could be assured it would not be tampered with. They were understandably suspicious of powerful interests seeking to re-write the narrative (this 'families first' principle is now followed by other inquiries and panels). We needed to agree a venue that would provide privacy for the families and protection from the glare of the media as they absorbed what we knew would be traumatic material. We consulted them, without disclosing the content of the report, discussed various options in the Panel, and finally settled on Liverpool Cathedral. It suited the complex logistical requirements and also provided a dignified and sacred place to remember and honour the 96.

Every day, for three months before we published the report on 12 September 2012, I read in my daily prayers one of the parables of Jesus, 'The widow and the unjust judge' in Luke's Gospel.

In a certain city there was a judge who neither feared God nor had respect for people. In that city there was a widow who kept coming to him and saying, 'Grant me justice

11

against my opponent.' For a while he refused; but later
he said to himself, 'Though I have no fear of God and no
respect for anyone, yet because this widow keeps bothering
me, I will grant her justice, so that she may not wear me out
by continually coming.' And the Lord said, 'Listen to what
the unjust judge says. And will not God grant justice to his
chosen ones who cry to him day and night?'
(Luke 18.2–7)

I used to think that this was a parable about prayer. In the
context of Hillsborough, I began to feel the force of it as an
allegory about justice. 'Grant me justice.' That had been the
prayer of the Hillsborough widows, mothers, fathers, sons and
daughters for over twenty years. As I read this parable each day,
I could see and feel so many dimensions of their search for justice: how easy it is to give up and to lose heart; how indifferent
the judicial system seems to ordinary people; the imbalance of
power in the relationships between the powerful and the powerless; the indomitable human spirit that refuses to give up. How,
in spite of the impossibly long wait needed until we see it, Jesus
says that God is on the side of those seeking justice. It was this
last point that fortified me.

I was very aware of how much Hillsborough was absorbing
my time and energy, and of how some in the diocese were now
commenting on how little they saw of me in the parishes. Was
it right for me to sacrifice so much pastoral and evangelistic
work in the cause of justice? This parable of Jesus helped me to
keep my hand to the plough and not look back. It is necessary
not to overlook but to act on the love and justice of God. What I
had to learn was that, although I had to withdraw from certain
activities in the diocese, the search for truth and justice was
profoundly pastoral, deeply evangelistic in the richest sense of
that word and a moral imperative.

Although we had made preparations to face the media, the source of my nerves on the morning of 12 September as we gathered in the cathedral was how I was going to be with the families. We knew that what was in the report would turn their world upside down. The emotional tension knotted every muscle. Grief is a contagion. I felt in my soul a suppressed weeping that I feared could erupt at any moment as I caught sight of the heavily lined faces of many of the 250 family members taking their seats in the Well of the cathedral. As a priest, you learn at such events to tighten the valve on your own feelings so as to lead others through the trauma of the occasion, and then find your own time and place to release your inner turmoil.

The Secretariat and the cathedral staff excelled in putting the families at the centre of all their planning. Everything possible was done to give them space and privacy and to put them at ease on such a stressful day. During the presentation of the report by the Panel, three family members fainted. A year later, Margaret Aspinall, recalled the day to me:

'Oh Bishop, we'll never forget those three words. They turned our world upside down.'

'What were those words, Margaret?' I struggled to remember.

'You said, 'You've all come here today wondering if we've found anything new,' and then you said, 'And we have'. And with those three words everything changed . . . and turned our world upside down.'

Phil Scraton and Bill Kirkup led the presentation. When Bill presented his analysis of the post-mortem reports, there were audible gasps from the families. At the end of the ninety-minute presentation and just before copies of the full report were given to each family, another leading family member took the microphone. We had no idea what he would say. From his trembling lips slipped the word, 'Sorry'. He had come forwards to apologize for ever doubting the integrity of the Panel.

It brought a lump to my throat. It's true that we had faced many challenges posed by the families and survivors, but on this day of truth-telling it was they who merited the apology, not us.

His 'sorry' spoke to me and my colleagues of the dignity and grace that seasoned the frustration and anger of their long struggle for truth and justice.

After the families had had time to read at least the summary of the report, we reconvened for a live video link to the House of Commons and a statement on Hillsborough by the Prime Minister, David Cameron. Unequivocally, he offered an apology to the families for 'a double injustice'. The day before, at 8.30 a.m., without actually giving him the report, I briefed him in his Downing Street office. He grasped the gravity immediately. He recognized the injustice of the 96 having been blamed for their own deaths, as well as the further injustice of having had to wait over twenty years for the truth to be told. If ever there were a case of 'justice delayed is justice denied', it was Hillsborough.

The rest of the day was taken up with press conferences by the Panel and by the families, and with an opportunity for the families to question Panel members both formally and informally.

At the end of the afternoon, at about 4.30, we gathered the families together to draw the lengthy proceedings to a close. It had been a momentous day. It was already making news around the world. For both families and survivors, it was bittersweet. They were vindicated at last and heartbroken, their grieving revived, their love rekindled, their loss magnified.

But if grief is a journey without destination, then on 12 September 2012 in Liverpool Cathedral, two milestones were reached, with the names of truth and justice, further memorials to the 96.

Throughout the day the chapter house, located to the left of the high altar, had been set aside as a chapel for the families to use as a retreat from the intensity of the proceedings. I thanked the families for their extraordinary forbearance through the long day. I said I was now going to the 'chapel' to remember the 96 and to pray to God that truth and justice would prevail in his world. I walked the length of the cathedral and knelt down in the bishop's stall with my face in my hands. For the next hour I think most of the 250 family members followed – some kneeling, some standing, some looking in the Book of Remembrance, some praying and all of us caught up in a physical and spiritual movement of to-ing and fro-ing, of reliving and remembering, of dying and living. Then, from within me sprang a tearful well, dampening my eyes in thanksgiving that on this day it was in the House of God that the families heard truth call out to and for justice. From that day on, words like these have leapt off the pages of the Bible for me: 'The works of His hands are truth and justice' (Psalm 111.7, Book of Common Worship).

On that first anniversary of the release of the Panel's report, when Margaret shared her recollections of the day, I told her how, every day for three months, I had read the parable of the widow and the unjust judge.

I reached for the little Bible in my briefcase and laid it between us. I opened it at Luke 18 and read it aloud to us both. Although I was reading it myself, I felt that I had never heard it spoken so poignantly or so powerfully. It was as if someone else was in the room reading it to us. Context is everything when reading the Bible – both the context in which the words were first written and the context in which they are heard and read.

The words, 'And will not God grant justice to those who ask' seemed to connect with Margaret's recollection of the three little words 'And we have'. To this day and for as long as I shall live, this story of Jesus is filed in my heart under 'Hillsborough'.

At the 27th anniversary, which the families thought should be the last act of remembrance for the 96 at Anfield, Margaret asked me to give the address. I had by then retired from being Bishop of Liverpool. With the blessing of my successor, I returned some four years after the publication of the Panel's report. The second inquests, which were already the longest in British legal history, were drawing to an end. Everyone had to be careful about what they said for fear of prejudice and contempt. I nevertheless felt free to tell the crowd how much that parable of Jesus had meant to me. I paraphrased it and said how this widow had come constantly pleading for justice but how she was continually let down by the judicial system. I paused and deliberately emphasized the next six words: '*but she would not give up*'. The story did not need to be expounded or explicitly applied. At these words, the crowd of some 20,000 began to stand and applaud. Here, on the terraces at Anfield, the creed they were cheering was the message of Jesus.

On the train home over the Pennines that evening, I mused in my thoughts to God about how, 2,000 years on, some 20,000 people had cheered one of Jesus' parables that encouraged the defiant and indefatigable pursuit of justice. Then my heart sank back in sadness. The Church now seemed increasingly remote from ordinary people who simply wanted to live in a fairer world.

In the Hillsborough narrative, there have been many remarkable figures. During my association with the families, three women featured prominently. Margaret Aspinall, the mother of James, as Chair of the HFSG, proved herself to be an exceptional orator at the anniversary services. I've been with her in meetings with Cabinet Ministers and Prime Ministers where she has spoken without fear. Ever since James was 'unlawfully killed', she has sought to hold to account those responsible. She has done it for James and for all the 96 with compassion, courage and a cast-iron determination.

Another mother, Anne Williams, came to prominence. She lost her son, Kevin, at Hillsborough. She campaigned until her dying day for the first coroner's verdict of accidental death to be overturned. Three times she pleaded for a fresh inquest, taking her case in the end to the European Court of Justice. Each time, her request was turned down, but she, too, 'would not give up'. By the time the Panel's report was published, Anne had been diagnosed with terminal cancer.

I shall never forget her countenance on the day. She was already showing the signs of her disease but, when she heard the outcome of the report, her whole appearance changed. It was as if she had been given a transfusion. She seemed to grow taller and there was light in her eyes and a radiance to her face. Vindication brings with it a special aura.

Shortly before Anne died, I was asked to visit her. For some time I had been thinking of giving to Margaret and to Anne personal gifts to express my appreciation of them both. As I stood in my study ahead of my visit, before me on the mantelpiece were three ornaments. In an instant, I knew – I just knew – that I had to take to Anne the marble pietà of Jesus being taken down from the cross and held by his mother. It had been given to me by my own mother some twenty years earlier on her return from a visit to Rome. My mother was now dead, and even though Anne was about to die and would have no long-term use for it, I was certain that this was the gift that I should bear.

When I arrived, we were left alone to talk. Anne knew that she was dying and death held no fear for her. It had no sting. She seemed to meet it as its victor, for this would be her gateway to being with Kevin again. She told me remarkable stories about supernatural manifestations that convinced her Kevin was in heaven. I asked her if she would like me to say a prayer with her but, before I did, I said that I had a gift for her.

She took it slowly and unwrapped it almost reverently, then looked at me and asked, 'How did you know?' 'How did I know what?' I replied gently. 'How did you know that the last gift Kevin gave me before he died was a miniature pietà he'd brought back from Rome?' Anne never lived to hear the jury return the determination of 'unlawful killing', but in her soul she already knew the truth. And the publication of the Panel's report had set her free.

Sheila Coleman was neither bereaved nor a survivor of Hillsborough, but for the tenure of the Panel took a leading role in speaking for the Hillsborough Justice Campaign, which represented the survivors, as well as a small group of the bereaved families. I gave Sheila a miniature of a sculpture that I had commissioned Stephen Broadbent to make for the chapel at Bishop's Lodge. It was of the figure of Christ bent out of metal and casting a shadow over the city and the River Mersey with words of Jesus around the glass circumference: 'If only you recognized the things that make for peace' (Luke 19.42). These had been spoken through tears as Jesus looked out over the city of Jerusalem. There can be no peace without justice - or, to put it another way, the degree to which a society can be at peace with itself is in direct proportion to the degree of fairness with which its members relate to one another.

In all the conversations that I've had since taking on Chair of the Panel, I often ask people for their own definition of justice. The one that speaks to me with the greatest challenge, however, comes not from a conversation, but from a fourth-century Christian philosopher from North Africa called Lactantius, in his *Divine Institutes*. I quoted it at the front of the Panel's report: 'The whole point of justice consists precisely in our providing for others through humanity what we provide for our own family through affection.' I know that this sets the bar very high, but it gives us the measure of how far we, as a society, have failed the families and survivors of the Hillsborough disaster.

When the new inquests began, the coroner, Sir John Goldring, invited all the families to offer pen portraits of their loved ones to the court. This humanized the legal proceedings and helped to undo the media stereotype of the 96 fans who had died. I was advised not to attend the inquests, since the judge rightly made it clear that the jury had to decide on the evidence laid before the court and not on previous investigations. Nevertheless, I followed events closely.

I was invited by Sir Keir Starmer, Director of Public Prosecutions, to chair a forum for the families at which they would be kept abreast of three separate processes: the criminal investigation by the police (known as Operation Resolve), the investigation into police conduct by the Independent Police Complaints Commission (now IOPC) and the assessment of the files by the Crown Prosecution Service. I was also retained by Home Secretary Theresa May to advise the Government on its own relationship with the families, to whom it had a duty of care following the Panel's report.

Keir Starmer showed empathy and flexibility in the formation of this forum, which would give the families confidence in the processes. The families were fearful that just as there had been push-back following the Taylor Report in 1990, so vested interests would mount fierce resistance to the Panel's report at the second set of inquests.

But it was Theresa May who made the most significant and far-reaching decision in the families' search for justice. At the original inquests, the families came to court without any assistance to pay for their legal representation and found themselves up against public authorities with expert legal support paid for by the State. Forty-three families clubbed together to pay for one barrister to act for them all. Such inequality of arms on such an unlevel playing field at contested inquests has a major impact on their outcome.

Theresa May recognized this injustice and ruled that the Government would not only fund the legal representation of the families but would also cap the amount of public money that the South Yorkshire Police could spend on their own legal costs. Mrs May gave Ken Sutton the task of devising a bespoke scheme, which he did with his colleague Andrew Hooper. This equality of arms made the playing field level and played a large part in having the original verdict of accidental death overturned, with the jury returning a determination of 'unlawful killing'. Parity between the parties in the court proved essential to justice.

There were many people who thought that the new determination would give the families 'closure' and bring an end to the whole matter. But, as one of the mothers had said to me, 'Once you know that your children have been unlawfully killed then you want to know who was responsible.' The families therefore followed very closely the subsequent criminal investigation that culminated in the trials of the match commander, David Duckenfield, and others. What the families and survivors wanted was not revenge but accountability; that after all these years and the legal reckoning of 'unlawful killing' someone should be held responsible. Justice required that the truth not only be told but also that it be owned. Without the ownership of truth through accountability, justice for the Hillsborough families would forever be delayed and denied.

I mentioned the ornaments on my study mantelpiece and the prominent women in the Hillsborough narrative. To Margaret Aspinall I gave a cross of nails. I had no box for it and sent it in an old cuff-link box. To my surprise, when I saw her on the day when the families heard that the jury could not agree on a verdict in the trial of David Duckenfield, Margaret took the box out of her handbag, opened it and showed me the cross. We were back in the Cunard Building, where the families were following the trial in Preston by video link. The mayor, Joe Anderson, allowed Margaret and me to talk privately in his office. Although it was the match commander who was on trial that day, Margaret said that ever since the 96 died, the families had felt that it was they who were on trial. Although after publication of the Panel's report, the South Yorkshire Police had issued a fulsome apology, and although at the second inquests the match commander had admitted his liability and apologized to the families, at the subsequent trials, the old discredited nostrums were repeated, impugning the integrity of the fans and the survivors. Margaret ran her fingers over the cross as she spoke. 'I take this everywhere with me, Bishop. Sometimes I have to go out of the room when I want to swear. I don't want to swear in front of the cross.'

Margaret always prefers to talk about accountability rather than justice. For her, justice would be the restoration of James to her, but that can never be, this side of eternity. One of the most harrowing conversations I have ever had in my life was listening to Margaret recount the moment in which she heard that James had been killed at Hillsborough. It is too holy a scene for me to describe even with her permission. I believe it is for her, and only her, to share.

The cross is a symbol of many things but, in Margaret's hands, it became for me an emblem of injustice. When Jesus told that story of a bereaved woman pleading for justice, perhaps he thought of his own mother, who would one day witness the unlawful killing of her son. I watched Margaret touch the cross tenderly.

Most recently, more than thirty years since the Hillsborough disaster, Margaret issued her own verdict to me: 'We're told that everyone is equal in the eyes of the law. It's not true. We're equal only in the eyes of God. In the eyes of the law we are definitely not equal.' That has been the experience of the Hillsborough families. The fact that it has taken so long to establish truth, accountability and justice is the greatest proof that delayed justice is the denial of justice.

When Theresa May was Home Secretary, she asked to meet the families. Before entering the room, I advised her that she was about to meet some of the most experienced lawyers in the country. 'They've not been to law school. They've not got law degrees but, over the years, they have built up a great deal of legal knowledge.' What they encountered over the decades was a lack of candour, a lack of equality and a lack of empathy. These deficiencies added further to a lack of justice. One of the reasons that Margaret and others struggle on so tenaciously is that they are not alone in this denial of justice: too many others have suffered from the same deficit of empathy, equality and candour. Margaret has always believed that the families' struggle is of national significance and relevance. As I have looked on, I have shared their disillusionment, especially when they have found that the very instruments of justice failed them.

The Hillsborough narrative is a canon of many stories in which the police, the courts, the lawyers and even the judiciary are often found wanting. To ordinary people who have a genuine grievance, they can seem to be a phalanx of frustration and obstruction. This is not to say that there are no good and honourable men and women within the judicial system.

There are. However, the system allows the less honourable to take advantage of that presumption of integrity which is indispensable to the administration of justice. It is something that requires urgent attention. Failure to address this blemish will continue to undermine trust in the institutions of justice and will have a deleterious effect on the stability and solidity of our society.

After the inquests, Theresa May commissioned from me a second report, which I entitled 'The patronising disposition of unaccountable power'. Its aim was to learn from what the families had gone through and to ensure that their perspective was not lost. I had the help of others, especially Neil Roberts, who had served with distinction in the Secretariat of the Panel, and we produced twenty-five points of learning and offered three major proposals to address the triple deficit of empathy, equality and candour that blights the judicial system.

The first was to produce the Charter for Families Bereaved through Public Tragedy. Public bodies that sign up to it commit to placing the public interest above their own reputation and to refusing to put their institution ahead of the needs, interests and rights of the victims of public tragedies. The charter also commits the organizations to submit to public scrutiny in an open and transparent way and to eschew any attempt to defend the indefensible. It also includes a refusal to disparage those who have suffered. It pledges to treat victims and the public with courtesy and respect. The Crown Prosecution Service has signed up to it, as have the Royal Borough of Kensington and Chelsea following the Grenfell disaster. The Government has indicated that it will respond to the report when the final Hillsborough trial is over. The families have welcomed the charter, which they feel would have made a difference to how they themselves were treated by the institutions on their long road to justice. The charter is an attempt to bring some empathy into the process of scrutinizing tragic events.

The second was to recommend that a way be found to establish parity in the Coroner's Court between a bereft family whose loved one has died at the hands of the State and the particular agency, be it, for example, the police, the prison service or a hospital trust. At the moment, a grieving family can find itself defenceless in a Coroner's Court, without any legal representation, facing a State agency and an expert legal team all funded by the public purse. It offends the principle of natural justice. Hitherto, the Government has refused to guarantee support for families at contested inquests, which amount to about 20 per cent of the total. It is hoped that recognizing the inequity and the iniquity of such a position will lead the Government one day to incorporate into its judicial reforms the groundbreaking precedent established by Theresa May. The charity Inquest has amassed enormous evidence that the present system is unjust and in need of reform.

The third is that there should be a duty of candour laid on the police when it comes to investigating their actions in dealing with public tragedies. This is crucial in giving confidence to victims. Time and again you hear, not just from the Hillsborough families but also from countless others, that public authorities, including the police, drag their feet when it comes to disclosing vital documents. I was shocked to discover that police files do not come under the Public Records Act. In fact, there is nothing in law to stop them from being destroyed at the whim of a senior officer. The National Police Chiefs Council recognizes the force of the argument and is currently reviewing its own policy. The Government will declare its own position after the last of the Hillsborough trials.

These three proposals have arisen out of the experiences of the Hillsborough families and the injustices that they have suffered. To take up Margaret Aspinall's acute observation, how do we translate a conviction that we are all equal in the sight of God into us all being equal in the eyes of the law? It is a moral question. It is a divine imperative.

As Jesus said, 'It behoves us not to overlook but to act upon the love and the justice of God' (Luke 11.42, my translation).

After more than thirty-two years, all the legal proceedings concerning the Hillsborough disaster have come to an end, with only one person found guilty of an offence under the Health and Safety Regulations and fined £6,500. For the families and survivors who have sought and continue to seek accountability rather than revenge, there is bitter disappointment and disillusionment with the judicial system. As Jenni Hicks told Judith Moritz, the BBC North of England correspondent, 'Something's got to change.' The failure to establish accountability for the tragic loss of the 96 does not detract from the established fact that they were 'unlawfully killed'. Nor does it change the fact that the Hillsborough Independent Panel found the police statements were altered in favour of themselves and against the fans and so altered the course of justice. Without the tenacity of the families, born out of their grief-stricken commitment to restore honour to their loved ones, which had been besmirched by the police and the press, there would not have been even this degree of truth and justice. The Hillsborough narrative is a saga of justice delayed, denied and discredited. The cry of the widow in the parable of Jesus, 'Grant me justice' still echoes around the memorial to the 96, now 97 with the death of Andrew Devine 32 years later.

Postscript

I was asked to provide the 'Thought for the Day' on the *Today* programme on BBC Radio 4 on both the twentieth and thirtieth anniversaries of the Hillsborough disaster. I reproduce here what I said on each occasion.

15 April 2009

Today marks the twentieth anniversary of the Hillsborough disaster. Thousands are expected to fill the stadium at Anfield this afternoon.

At six minutes past three the crowd will fall silent. That was the time, twenty years ago, when the referee blew the whistle to stop the FA Cup semi-final between Liverpool and Nottingham Forrest that had only just begun at the Hillsborough Stadium in Sheffield. Although more than 1,100 police officers were on duty and 44 ambulances were in attendance, they were to no avail as thousands of Liverpool fans were fed into already over-crowded stands. And 96 people, men, women and children were crushed to death.

Twenty years on, the pain remains. Although Lord Justice Taylor's inquiry was clear about where the responsibility for the disaster lay, no prosecutions ever followed, which left the families feeling doubly aggrieved.

Yet these families have carried their sorrow with extra-ordinary dignity. They do not hide their wounds, but neither do they parade them for sympathy. The scars are simply part of who they now are. They are there, too, in the body of the wider community. For it's the crosses we bear as much as the joys of life's triumphs that give a person and a community their character.

One of the thought-provoking aspects of the resurrection of Jesus is the way he presents himself to his followers, scars and all. There's no attempt on his part to hide his wounds. There's certainly no supernatural surgery that erases the mutilation of his crucifixion. His damaged, tortured, humiliated body is there for all to see after his death.

Just a few days ago, I was with a mother who had lost her two teenagers at Hillsborough. I say 'lost' but, in fact, her testimony was that they were still with her. I know this may sound fanciful to some, maybe even wishful thinking to others, but it will ring true to many who are tragically bereaved.

You might think that the terrifying circumstances of their cruel deaths would drive the bereaved to banish for ever all thought of their suffering from mind and heart. Not so. As with the wounds of Christ, the scars, now sacred, endear the beloved to the bereaved and make them ache to remember.

As surely as they do in Dunblane and Hungerford, in Aberfan and now in L'Aquila in Italy. And as we shall certainly do today in Liverpool. Before the names of those who died are read, the stands will echo with the singing of 'Abide with me'. It's sung on many great occasions but seldom will the last verse be sung with such poignancy.

> Hold thou thy cross before my closing eyes;
> Shine through the gloom, and point me to the skies;
> Heaven's morning breaks, and earth's vain shadows flee;
> In life, in death, O Lord, abide with me.

15 April 2019

Today is the thirtieth anniversary of the Hillsborough disaster. The tremors of the tragedy shook the nation. But that's all that can be said for now because the trials are ongoing.

This past weekend also saw the anniversary of the Jallianwala Bagh massacre in Amritsar, which happened tragically one hundred years ago on Palm Sunday. These and the anniversaries of other public tragedies raise the question as to whether there can ever be closure for those traumatized by such disasters.

Having chaired the Hillsborough Independent Panel and the Gosport Independent Panel, I've been approached by some of the survivors of the Grenfell Tower fire and also by the communities affected by the contaminated blood scandal. These are all subject to various judicial processes.

Those who look on these events from afar often ask me about what the families are after and if it's closure that they're seeking. I can't speak for any of those caught up in these tragedies, but the more I've immersed myself in their stories, the more reticent I've become about answering the question.

To be honest, whatever happens in and to the various judicial processes of inquests and trials, inquiries and panels I don't think there's ever such a thing as closure. Why? Because there can never be, nor should there ever be, closure to the commitment you have to someone you love and have lost. There may be closure to the judicial process but not to the emotions.

Grief is a journey without destination. There are many milestones along the way when you stop and think of what might have been and what should have been. But as you travel through grief, you're not looking for a signpost that reads 'The End'. There's no finish to the cherishing of someone you love.

This week traces the events leading up to Easter – the betrayal, trial, torture and execution of Jesus. It's the very opposite of closure. Holy Week is designed to keep alive the memory of Jesus, who countered closure by telling his followers to keep remembering him. For two thousand years, Christians have refused to call closure on the death of Christ. It's not a morbid obsession, but the cherishing of a life well lived though cruelly cut short. Holy Week is a defiant remembrance of the injustice that killed him, a symbol of all the injustices that have ever trammeled the goodness of the world.

And closure is not an option when the one you love calls out to be remembered.

2

The city

I had never been to Hull when, in 1994, out of the blue, I received a letter from the Archbishop of York, John Habgood, asking me to meet him as he was looking to advise the Prime Minister and the Queen on the appointment of the next Bishop of Hull. At that time I was the vicar of Emmanuel Church, South Croydon, a caring, active and growing congregation always looking for new ways to serve the community of its suburban parish.

After my interview with the Archbishop I met the Archdeacon of the East Riding, Hugh Buckingham, who drove me to Hull. We parked by a tall monument. 'Who's that?' I asked. 'That's William Wilberforce!' he said, almost triumphantly and certainly proudly.

His enthusiasm matched my own. Ever since my days as a student, William Wilberforce had been for me the model of a great life. His faith was evangelical and the source of his conviction to enter public life. He became MP for Hull and fought for the abolition of the slave trade and, eventually, of slavery itself. His politics were informed by his reading of the Bible. He was convinced that a moral life in both the private and public domains was the key to a harmonious society. But as he surveyed 'the European nations' at the beginning of the nineteenth century, he concluded that 'it was a selfish, a luxurious, an irreligious, and an inconsiderate world.'

Without specifying the evil of slavery, he put his finger on society's malaise: 'We are so slow in giving ear to what conscience urges us . . . so dexterous in justifying what is clearly wrong, in palliating what we cannot justify.' How else could the so-called civilized world justify the barbarous trade of slaves? Wilberforce was highly critical of those in public life and even more scathing about the quality of the Christian religion being pedalled by its bishops and clergy. The only way forward into the nineteenth century was, he believed, to call for a spiritual and moral transformation in the upper echelons of society. This he did in a book with the snappy title *A Practical View of the Prevailing Religious System of Professed Christians in the Upper and Middle Classes of this Country Compared with Real Christianity*. He excoriated the hypocrisy of both civic and religious leaders. In a highly personal passage, he urged on them spiritual and moral renewal under the title 'Looking unto Jesus'. In *A Practical View* (1836, Henry Washbourne), he notes that this inner transformation would lead to:

> peace with all . . . as members of the same family, entitled not only to the debts of justice, but to the less definite and more liberal claims of fraternal kindness; all would be active and harmonious . . . the whole machine of civil life would work without obstruction or disorder and the course of its movements would be like the harmony of the spheres.

The fact that Wilberforce was buried in Westminster Abbey alongside prime ministers was a measure of his stature as a politician and statesman. Although he never held high office, according to William Hague, his biographer, 'his achievements were greater than those of most of the occupants of the highest offices in the land'. Hague adds:

> He showed how a political career could be conducted differently, pursuing long-term objectives deeply rooted

in certain principles, strengthened in his indifference to holding power by his understanding of its transitory nature. As a result he went to his grave fulfilled by the knowledge of what he had helped to do while those politicians to whom power alone is important decline in their old age into 'bitterness and despair'.

Wilberforce, in spite of fierce opposition from his family, was from an early age influenced by evangelical Christianity, which grew out of a reaction against the nominal religion of a corrupt Church. It is thought that much of the social reform in the nineteenth century was a product of the growing evangelical movement led by the likes of Elizabeth Fry and Lord Shaftesbury. The word 'evangelical' has since fallen on hard times, discredited by some of our transatlantic cousins, but in the nineteenth century, its hallmarks were personal goodness and social harmony through both generous philanthropy and radical new laws.

Legislation such as the Factory Act of 1833, drafted to give protection to children, was fiercely resisted both inside and outside Parliament by critics accusing reformers of destabilizing the economy and of 'ruining the empire', a charge laid against Wilberforce and others as they championed the abolition of the slave trade in 1807 and the abolition of slavery (achieved in 1833 also).

Although we live in a very different age, I have admired the example of Wilberforce and sought to embrace his brand of Christianity, which was characterized by personal spiritual renewal, through 'looking unto Jesus', and by the undoing of injustice through both charitable activity and legislative reform. Arriving in Hull, the city of William Wilberforce, as its bishop in 1994 was to put all this to the test by trying to practise what he preached.

I was ordained bishop in York Minster in November 1994 and celebrated my first Easter in Beverley Minster the following April. The vicar gave all the children Cadbury Creme Eggs when they came to the altar rail. There were twenty-five left over after the service and I asked if I could take them with me to an all-age Easter service I was doing that afternoon on the Longhill Estate. The church there had been closed following a scandal regarding child abuse. Since then, the church community had been kept alive by a passionately committed youth worker called Marianne.

She asked me to lead an informal Communion service for children and adults in the church hall, which doubled as a second-hand clothes shop and community centre. Twenty-five children with as many adults arrived at the hall. We stood in a circle for the short service. Marianne asked if Stacey, a seven-year-old who had been brought by her grandmother, could read two prayers she had written. I readily agreed. I began by saying that I was sorry for what had happened in the past and for the fact that the church had remained closed. We sang, we prayed, we shared the bread with the children and distributed the little Easter eggs. I was just about to say the blessing when Marianne appeared at my side to rebuke me for not calling Stacey forward. I asked Stacey to stand by me and she prayed aloud two beautiful prayers. Six weeks later, she was murdered in her own home when a man known to her mother threw a petrol bomb through the letter-box. The firemen brought her two brothers out screaming, but Stacey was cradled in the fireman's arms and silent. Her burns were so severe that she could not feel them. She died a few days later. I was asked to take her funeral. When I went to visit the family to plan the service I found that everything I had ever learnt about ministering to the bereaved turned to dust.

The road to the cemetery chapel was lined with thousands of people. Stacey's head teacher described her as 'an angel on loan from heaven' and they played her favourite song, Michael Jackson's 'Heal the world'. With the opening lines:

> Think about the generations and say that we want to make it a better place for our children and our children's children, so that they know it's a better world for them, and think, if they can make it a better place.

A few months earlier, my own children and my wife had nearly been killed when, at a T-junction, a lorry sliced off the bonnet of our car. A few weeks previously, I had fitted the car with expensive new tyres with a premonition that, in the winter months and in a new city, safety would be paramount. It was my wife Sarah's quick reaction, combined with the grip of the tyres, that saved them from the main impact. The police rang me to tell me to go straight to the hospital. I passed them on the way. The children were standing by the roadside, crying, as Sarah, with a bloody and bandaged head, was being lifted into the ambulance. Our children survived, but Stacey died and, whichever way I looked at it, their lives were worlds apart. Neither they nor she was immune to suffering, but Stacey was infinitely more vulnerable and at risk in a manifestly unfair world where the streets were laid down on a foundation of injustice beneath a surface of good intentions.

> Yes, Oh God. Heal the world. Make it a better place. For Christ's sake. And for Stacey's. 'Let justice roll down like waters, and righteousness like an ever-flowing stream'. (Amos 5.24)

Up until that point, the emphasis in my own faith had been the leading of others to a transforming experience of Jesus. But I could now see more clearly the other side of the coin – the imperative to make the world a better and a fairer place.

33

At a recent speech day at Balcarras Academy, near Cheltenham, I was asked to give out the prizes and address the school leavers. Conscious of the gap between my generation and theirs, I was nervous. I told them I was there not to tell them to follow their dreams, nor to urge them to be the best possible person they could be. I said I had a simple message that would not make them famous, rich or popular: 'As you go through life, be fair, and so make the world a fairer place.' I was taken by surprise by the way they applauded. Here were young people cheering a recurrent theme from the beginning to the end of the Bible: 'What does the LORD require of you but to do justice, and to love kindness, and to walk humbly with your God?' (Micah 6.8). In other words, 'Be fair.'

In Hull, I began to immerse myself in the regeneration of the city, a path that I stuck to when, after four years there, my family and I were called to Liverpool where I became bishop in 1998. Liverpool and Hull faced very similar challenges as they made the transition from being wealthy ports of the eighteenth and nineteenth centuries into European cities of the digital twenty-first century.

We had been in Hull barely three years when I was asked to take on the role of Bishop of Liverpool. This would be our fourth home, and the girls' fourth school, in eight years. Sarah and I at first said no. Hull was about to celebrate its 800th anniversary and the future there was full of promise. Church and State, however, were finding it difficult to make the appointment to Liverpool and when I declined the offer, both Downing Street and Lambeth Palace pressed Sarah and me to reconsider. In the end, it was our eldest daughter Harriet who persuaded us. When we explained to the children why we kept going off into a huddle, Harriet made us think again with a simple question: 'If God is calling us shouldn't we go?'

To announce my appointment as Bishop of Liverpool, we chose the setting of the regenerated Albert Dock, wanting a backdrop that reflected the renewal of the city. The photographer of one national newspaper asked instead for a picture of me standing at a derelict site. It is difficult to defy media stereotypes.

In spite of the sophistication of the technology that they use, the media can seldom handle more than one message about any particular subject. The truth about Liverpool (as well as Hull) is that, although it is a city of great promise, both economically and culturally, which rewards private investment, it is also a city with huge challenges of deprivation and inequality, and merits investment from the public purse. Both messages are vital to its future. The stereotype does a disservice not just to the image but also to the people themselves, as it deprives the city of investment. The press officer declined the derelict site and there was no picture to accompany the article in that paper, but we agreed that no picture was better than the wrong picture.

In preparing to go to Liverpool, I was intrigued by the city's Latin motto, 'Deus nobis haec otia fecit' (God has bestowed these blessings upon us). It is from one of the poems by Virgil, the Roman poet, and comes from a conversation where a rich man is boasting of his wealth and explaining the source of his good fortune. Understandably, his interlocutor asks, who is this god who has given him all these blessings? The answer is revealing. It says everything about Liverpool's self-perception in the eighteenth and nineteenth centuries. The wealthy man names his divine benefactor as 'a city men call Rome'. The leaders of the city of Liverpool, which was the Heathrow of the nineteenth century, saw themselves at the centre of an empire.

Far from being the second city after London, they saw Liverpool as the new Rome and the fulcrum of the nation's wealth, leveraging international trade and commerce. The motto was powerfully expounded by the building of St George's Hall, perhaps the finest example of neoclassical architecture in Europe, decorated with statues of the 'city fathers' draped in Roman togas. But by the end of the twentieth century, Britain's Rome had fallen from its pedestal. Liverpool had lost half its population, with barely half a million left in the city to sustain all its grand buildings and parks.

Many cities like Hull and Liverpool now suffer from urban diabetes. There are often prestigious galleries, museums and concert halls in the centre, with gated apartments around docks (now marinas and smart shopping malls), while on the outer estates of social housing there's a different life being lived. Wealth is pumped, like blood, around the heart of the city, but fails to flow to the outer reaches, which atrophy and die. Beneath the signs of physical inequality evident in the consolidated poverty of bad housing, boarded-up shops, vandalized parks, high unemployment, low educational results and poor health statistics, there lies an inequality of esteem and aspiration. Low self-esteem and low aspiration militate against any plans to make a place better.

In my years of working with local people to regenerate their communities and to make them better places in which to live and work, another division emerged: one of images. In the long and many discussions between government agencies and local people, I began to notice the difference in the words that were used. Those who controlled the purse strings and prescribed top-down solutions addressed the issues of injustice with mechanical language. They talked of levers, triggers, buttons, targets and outcomes. Yet those who lived in the communities and wanted to be involved in improving them used organic language like sowing seeds, planting and branching out.

The people often felt overwhelmed and, sometimes, oppressed by the mechanical approach, so that although the intention was to create a more just society, the actual process, with its imbalance of power, felt anything but fair.

In the early years of the New Deal for Communities programme, we received a visit from a team of senior civil servants from London to talk about the funding. I'd been asked to chair the board of the company set up to oversee the regeneration of the area, to which I'd agreed, provided it had the support of the community members who were all sitting alongside me. The officials started to lecture us about how 'we have given you all this money', as if it were their own personal largesse.

The tone was high-handed and patronizing and silenced the voices of the community board members, which took a lot of doing in that part of the city, where it was not unknown for people to turn up to public meetings with a megaphone to be sure of a hearing! The saddest part is that the officials probably didn't realize how patronizing they were being. That lack of awareness was all part of the imbalance of power and the unevenness of the relationship. This subtle intimidation further eroded the self-confidence of local people and added to their low self-esteem and low aspirations.

At the outset of the New Deal programme, we held a number of popular meetings in the Kensington area of Liverpool to name the strengths and weaknesses of the community and to identify the challenges and the opportunities. Some of the most energetic and committed activists were young mothers who wanted a better life for their children. One major concern that emerged was that there was no secondary school in the area. When children left the care of their primary schools and were bussed out of this network of guardianship into different secondary schools around the city, they became vulnerable to other influences, such as drugs, gangs and petty crime. 'Why don't you ask for a secondary school?' I asked. 'This New Deal programme is about putting you in the driving seat.' Their answer was revealing: 'We'd never be allowed it'.

This spoke of their lack of self-confidence and how they felt robbed of the power to make a difference to their world. As it happened, they did ask for one and they got one! Their plans coincided with the national City Academy initiative, which allowed the Church of England Diocese and the Roman Catholic Archdiocese of Liverpool to work together with the local community to build one of the first city academies, which fundamentally changed for the better the life chances of thousands of young people.

What became obvious to me was that the people not only knew their own problems but were also clear about some of the solutions. The intervention that was needed was not one of showering money on regeneration consultants. It was one of local people having access to power and irrigating the neighbourhood with the available money so that they could shape their own future. I could see that my own involvement as chair of the board could be part of that redistribution of power to the people.

A bishop in the Church of England occupies a unique position in the community. He or she is not simply a faith leader but also a civic leader. This arises out of the theology and history of the Church, as well as the constitution of the nation. Theologically, parish priests and bishops see themselves caring not just for members of their congregations but also for everybody who lives within their parish or diocese, whether they attend church services or not. The first question that ministers will ask when someone seeks their help is not, 'Do you come to church?' but 'Where do you live?' And if you live within that corner of God's kingdom for which they are responsible pastorally, you have a claim on their care.

Historically, the Church has stood at the centre of the community's life. Although that presence is no longer as bright as it was in the Middle Ages, there are still vestiges of it to varying degrees of strength across the country in church schools, youth groups, food banks, credit unions, care for the elderly and memorial services after tragedy. The thousands of historic buildings are also testament to the influence the Church has had on our culture. Our language, literature, laws, liberty, learning and landscape all bear the hallmarks of how the Christian faith has helped to make the nation.

Constitutionally, that influence is symbolized by the public role the Church of England continues to have in our common civic life through national commemorations, especially in St Paul's Cathedral and Westminster Abbey. It also finds expression in the presence of twenty-six bishops in the House of Lords, who sit there alongside their peers as elders of our society, helping to refine legislation in light of their pastoral experience. Whatever the rights and wrongs of how this role has evolved and should continue to evolve, the fact is that it bestows on a bishop what some would call 'soft power' and a degree of access to those in power. I found that, in my various commitments in Liverpool, I was able to use that opportunity to empower those alongside whom I was working. Two episodes, which happen to be connected to the academy, stand out in my memory.

Once we had agreed as a board to petition for a new school, it fell to me as chair to meet with the Chief Executive of Liverpool City Council. A shrewd and tough negotiator, he marshalled all the arguments to prove that the city did not need another secondary school. I stood my ground and rehearsed all the arguments that had come out of the community consultation. When I realized that I was getting nowhere, I fired a parting shot: 'Well, you might as well send in the bulldozers and flatten the place!' To the Chief Executive's credit, he changed his mind and, in the end, did everything it took to make it happen. And it did.

The second episode that will remain with me came after we were told that we could go ahead and build the city academy. We were also informed that we had first to raise two million pounds and that, for this, we could not use public money. This was a huge blow to our confidence and dented our enthusiasm.

One of the issues on Merseyside is that the wealth which sailed in and out of Liverpool and built the city, literally on the backs of slaves in the eighteenth and nineteenth centuries, had drained away from the north to the south. Raising both public and private investment is a constant challenge. In order to raise the two million pounds, either we would have to ask a lot of people for a little money or a few people for a lot. Because of my own role both locally and nationally, it fell to me to secure the funding and to concentrate on approaching a carefully selected handful of philanthropists.

In my very first meeting with a trustee of a seriously endowed trust, I confess to almost kneeling on the velvet carpet of his office in Knightsbridge, a stone's throw away from Kensington in London, and begging him to support our vision for a city academy in a very different Kensington in Liverpool. The trust gave the proposed academy half a million pounds!

To be the bearer of good news to others is the happiest of human experiences. I could not wait to tell my colleagues on the board. They could hardly believe it. Nor could I! Some years later, that same trustee was visiting Liverpool on another matter and dropped by unannounced to see the academy. Sitting on the wall in their tartan uniforms were two senior girls, who stood up as we approached. When asked what they were hoping to do when they left school, one said she wanted to be a journalist; the other said she was hoping to become a solicitor. What aspiration! What self-esteem!

In one of the predecessor schools, 27 per cent of pupils had achieved five GCSEs at grades A to C; within eight years, the academy achieved 97 per cent. As the teller of this story, I know that the achievement belongs to very many people. I know, too, that such attainment is also and always fragile. I know, too, more clearly in retrospect, what my own particular contribution was. It was about using the power vested in my own position, for theological, historical and constitutional reasons, and sharing it with those who had little or none of it.

The Church is not just ambivalent about power; it is often positively hostile towards it, and many of its preachers make a virtue of powerlessness. But when you pay close attention to the controversial life of Jesus, you find that he was an immensely powerful figure. It is true that he held no position of power within the structures of his society. It is true that he often pitted himself against the institutionally powerful. But he also knew how to hold his listeners spellbound. He knew how to silence his critics. He could heal the sick, raise the dead, clear and clean a guilty conscience, and make a man part with his money. He was powerful and he knew how to use it – for good. Life itself is power. Just a blade of grass shooting up from the earth is life and power.

Once, in Jerusalem, after Jesus had healed a blind man, he found himself in an argument with religious leaders. They resented his power and his popularity. His retort was that he had come so the people might have life and have it in abundance (John 9—10). If we recognize that life is power, it adds a new dimension to that saying of Jesus. He throws down the gauntlet to anyone with any degree of power to use it justly for a fairer society.

As I have pondered all of this and wonder about those who may read these words, I would urge you not to be falsely modest about the power you possess and not to pretend that you are one of the powerless, or that you long to be divested of what power you hold. On the contrary, have a sober assessment of the power that is yours, be it position, influence, wealth, health, time, intelligence, energy or simply life itself, and consciously share it with those whose existence could be less deprived if you were honest about your influence and determined to use it for their benefit. I believe that this is what Wilberforce did. If everybody in any city consciously sought to use whatever power they had to improve the lot of those who had little, less or none, it would hasten the coming of a fairer world. But truly empowering the powerless means that those with power will have less of it at the end of the process. Perhaps that's why we find it so hard to do!

Striving for a just society is not only about changing structures. Vital though this is, the danger is that it puts achieving such an ideal beyond the reach of the individual. But if justice is about power and power is about life, then it involves us all at a personal level. Every individual and willful act of fairness contributes to making the world a fairer place. Using whatever life and power we possess to be fair in our dealings with others makes for a more just world. There is no human on the face of this earth who does not understand the moral imperative of these two monosyllabic words: 'Be fair.'

Postscript

'Thought for the Day', 31 January 2000

Lord Rogers has brought out his report on urban renaissance; the Government will soon bring out its white paper on the future of our cities; and the picture that comes to my mind is of Jesus approaching Jerusalem and weeping over the city, saying: 'If only you knew the things that made for peace . . . .' What brought tears to his eyes was their blindness, the failure to see the true solution to their problems.

The Prime Minister has set up social exclusion projects in seventeen cities around the country. And I declare an interest.

I've been asked to chair the regeneration company here in Liverpool. It covers the area of Kensington, which could not be more different from its namesake in London.

My first meeting was with a dozen local residents. They told me of murders, rapes and arson attacks in nearby streets in previous months. And Liverpool's no different from any other major European city. They said how powerless they felt when housing associations put in tenants who residents knew would wreck the neighbourhood. And an old lady told how one day she was walking down the street and two young men rammed her repeatedly with an empty supermarket trolley.

She rose up in her chair and said, 'I told them, "You are bullies and cowards, I'm not afraid of you. I've got so much anger inside of me I could floor the both of you".' She didn't say what happened next, but if I were them, I'd have legged it. She then crumpled in her chair and turned to me and pleaded, 'Help us, Bishop. Help us.'

What impresses me is the determination, especially of old people, who've lived in a place all their life, to stay. What encourages me is the ideas that local people have for making Kensington a better place. What humbles me is their commitment to turn it around. What inspires me is the belief that God is here – explicitly in the churches, and implicitly in all the hopes and plans that are coming from local people that will make for peace in this community.

So often urban regeneration has been top-down instead of bottom-up. Glossy brochures from consultants have dropped like confetti on our cities, drowning out the voices and aspirations of ordinary people who live there. Regeneration's got to be more than throwing money at buildings; it's about changing the hearts of two young men, and what they do with an empty supermarket trolley.

3

The Earth

In the millennium year, in the weeks leading up to Easter, I travelled in and around Liverpool, meeting as many young people as possible. In the secondary schools, I asked them to tell me about their dreams for and fears about the future, and I shared with them why I thought the message of Jesus was still on point 2,000 years later. I showed them a video about the threats to the planet and asked, on a scale of zero to ten, how worried were they about the future of the world? Zero was 'not bothered'; ten was 'really concerned'. I asked for a show of hands if they'd placed themselves between five and ten. In each school, sometimes in an assembly of 250 young people, every hand went up. It showed how, even twenty years before she arrived on the scene, the upcoming generation was such fertile ground for the message of Greta Thunberg. I then asked them to what extent should we do something about it? Some 98 per cent of the hands went up indicating agreement between five and ten on my scale. I came away from those encounters more challenged than challenging, and began to think through my own attitude to the Earth. I began to ponder the difference in attitudes to the environment between the generations and what is known as 'intergenerational justice', captured by the African proverb 'We have borrowed the present from our children.' Sustainability requires us to balance our own needs with the needs of future generations.

I discovered that there are those who question the whole concept of intergenerational justice on the grounds that those who have not yet been born cannot be said to have equivalent rights that can be set alongside those of people who are already alive. If morality were purely anthropocentric, it would be difficult to swat away such an argument. If, however, morality is rooted in some transcendent accountability that spans time and space, then the moral quality of our actions is measured by what is just in and to every generation.

The young people also sent me on another journey, which was to ask more searchingly if I could find anything in the teaching of Jesus about the Earth and environmental justice. If this was a pressing question for Christians at the dawn of the present millennium, it is an even more urgent question as I write now. Both former President Trump of the USA, with his denial of the science relating to climate change, and President Bolsonaro of Brazil, with his encouragement of those ravaging the Amazon rainforest, came to power with the pivotal support of evangelical Christians, who interpret the Bible literally. Coming from the British evangelical tradition, which takes the Scriptures as authoritative in understanding the ethos and the ethics of the Christian faith, I felt and continue to feel a special responsibility to unearth what the Bible really teaches us about environmental justice.

In my studies, I sought also to find out what the Jewish and Muslim ethics of the environment were. I enlisted on a course about Muslim theology and went to see the Chief Rabbi, the late Lord Jonathan Sacks. When I ventured that Jews might begin with the book of Genesis and God granting the human family dominion over the Earth, he stopped me.

'No, James. That's a very Christian way of reading the Bible on this subject! No,' he repeated, 'we start in the book of Deuteronomy with God's instruction to Moses that, as they entered the promised land, they were never to destroy a fruit-bearing tree.' Long before anyone knew the science of climate change, there was a religious intuition that trees were central to our ecology for both present and future generations.

As I shared with him the thrust of my study, which was to find out what, if anything, Jesus had to say about the Earth, he drew my attention to something that I already knew but had overlooked. The title that Jesus used more than any other to define his mission was 'Son of Man', which in Hebrew is 'Ben Adam', which literally means 'child of the one hewn from the Earth'. The rabbi opened my eyes to seeing Jesus in a completely new light and to understanding some of his sayings as if I had never read them before, not least two of his most famous: the Sermon on the Mount and the Lord's Prayer. Both speak about the Earth.

At the heart of the Lord's Prayer is the petition, 'Thy will be done in earth as it is in heaven'. It is a prayer for the earthing of heaven, for the grounding of God's values in the Earth. I prefer this old version to the modern translation, 'Your will be done on earth as it is in heaven'. I like the preposition 'in'. It speaks of God's will being done not just on the surface of the Earth but also deep within its ecology. The second saying, the Sermon on the Mount, has as its third blessing, 'Blessed are the meek, for they will inherit the earth' (Matthew 5.5). The importance of this blessing is that Jesus promised a future for the Earth, one that would be inherited by the meek, who tread the Earth and treat others with humility. The Lord's Prayer and the Sermon on the Mount express Jesus' conviction that the future will see a renewed and transformed Earth. Jesus believed that, at some stage after his death and resurrection from the dead, he, as the Child of the Earth, would, at the end of history, return in some glorious way to herald in 'the renewal of all things' (Matthew 19.28). Jesus, the Child of the Earth, would be the agent not of the Earth's obliteration, but of its regeneration.

There's a unique collection of sayings in the Gospels in which Jesus talks about himself as the Child of the Earth and in the same breath speaks about the Earth itself. For example, 'Just as Jonah was in the belly of the whale three days and three nights so the Child of the Earth will be in the heart of the Earth' (Matthew 12.40, my translation).' This is Jesus alluding to his own death and burial.

When they crucified him, before laying him in the heart of the Earth, the earth quaked. Then, when he was lifted out of the grave where he had been buried in the heart of the Earth, the earth quaked again.

In Jerusalem, in the Church of the Holy Sepulchre, on a level beneath the altar that marks the site of the crucifixion, there's an opening: through it you can see and feel the cleft in the rock left by the earthquakes. The quaking of the earth underlines the belief of many Christians that Jesus came to save not just individuals but also the whole of God's creation. The Earth could not keep silent at the life-giving death and resurrection of her own Child of the Earth, who had come down from heaven. In his hands, the Earth has a future.

In his poem 'God's grandeur', Gerard Manley Hopkins challenges all those who feel pessimistic about the future of the Earth. He acknowledges that all has been 'seared with trade; bleared, smeared with toil', but then adds, 'And for all this nature is never spent'.

There's no doubt that, in the history of the world, nature has never been so tested, but the Christian faith doubts that God will ever be content to give up on all he has made. I recall a lecture by Satish Kumar telling us that the word 'nature' comes from the Latin word 'to be born', and whatever is born breathes. Therefore, everything that has breath is not just part of nature but is also nature itself. When, at the end of the last psalm in the Bible, it says, 'Let everything that breathes praise the LORD!' (Psalm 150.6), the psalmist is calling on the whole of nature to praise God through its very being. The worship of God the Creator is not confined to humanity, but extends to every creature and to the whole of nature, of which the human family is a part.

When God made us in the divine image and gave us 'dominion', it was not to rape the Earth but to serve, conserve and sustain it with the same goodness and love out of which he made it and sustains us. If that's the vision of the Old Testament, then the lens is adjusted further by the New Testament, as it brings into sharper focus the role of Jesus in the formation of the world. The beginning of John's Gospel, in a passage made famous in the UK by the Christmas Festival of Nine Lessons and Carols as broadcast from King's College Cambridge, states that, 'All things came into being through him, and without him not one thing came into being' (John 1.3). Those are breathtaking words with which to describe any human being! St Paul went further and added his own understanding that 'all things have been created through him and for him' (Colossians 1.16). Never have two prepositions, 'through' and 'for', carried so much weight philosophically and theologically. In aligning Jesus with God the Creator, the first Christians were laying the foundations of a new environmental ethic. To rape the Earth, to spoil the soil, to abuse any of God's creatures, the birds of the air and the fish of the seas, to desecrate God's creation, was not just a crime against humanity and future generations, it was also a blasphemy, for it was to undo God's creative work in, through and for Christ.

Bless the LORD, O my soul.
O LORD my God, you are very great . . .
You set the earth on its foundations,
so that it shall never be shaken.
You cover it with the deep as with a garment;
the waters stood above the mountains . . .
giving drink to every wild animal;
the wild asses quench their thirst.

The Earth

By the streams the birds of the air have their habita-
    tion;
they sing among the branches.
From your lofty abode you water the mountains;
the earth is satisfied with the fruit of your work.
You cause the grass to grow for the cattle,
and plants for people to use,
to bring forth food from the earth,
and wine to gladden the human heart,
oil to make the face shine,
and bread to strengthen the human heart . . .
People go out to their work
and to their labour until the evening.
O LORD, how manifold are your works!
In wisdom you have made them all;
the earth is full of your creatures . . .
These all look to you
to give them their food in due season;
when you give to them, they gather it up;
when you open your hand, they are filled with good
    things.
When you hide your face, they are dismayed;
when you take away their breath, they die
and return to their dust.
When you send forth your spirit, they are created;
and you renew the face of the ground . . .
Bless the LORD, O my soul.
Praise the Lord!
(Psalm 104.1, 5–6, 11–15, 23–24, 27–30, 35, Book of
Common Prayer)

Very early one morning as the sun was rising over La Mosquitia
rainforest in Honduras, I rose from my log cabin, showered

under a bucket of cold water, walked down to the Patuca River with my Bible, which fell open at this psalm, and read it over and over again surrounded by chickens, goats, dogs, flies, spiders and countless other creatures, conscious that, even though nature can be 'red in tooth and claw', there was a harmony in this creation that was embracing me. Every verse seemed to vibrate in my soul.

I was in the country as a vice-president of Tearfund, an international development agency that my wife Sarah had helped to set up thirty years previously. We were the guests of Osvaldo Munguia, who, at great risk to his own safety, was resisting illegal logging and helping the forest communities to live sustainably. Osvaldo planted many seeds in my soul. We spent several days sailing up the Patuca River in a dugout canoe, visiting the villages deep in the forest. We had beans for breakfast, beans for lunch and beans for supper, with all the healthy consequences! The villagers held the forest in common and lived off the land. Osvaldo was helping them to learn how to do so sustainably.

There were two episodes that formed a bond between us. The first was a heart-to-heart conversation in which he talked humbly and passionately about the injustices being inflicted on the people by the logging companies, both legal and illegal, and by the government and international agencies, which were pressuring them into privatizing and selling off their land. Courageously, he encouraged the people to resist. His life was threatened but, intuitively, he knew that, in the name of justice, he had to continue his struggle to protect the forest for the sake of the people and their livelihood. It was their life. I had recently written a book called *Jesus and the Earth* (SPCK, 2003) and with it and my little Bible, showed him how what he was doing was walking in the footsteps of Jesus, earthing heaven by bringing good news to the poor. Scales seemed to fall from his eyes. Even though he had been brought up with the Bible, he had never made the connection between his intuitive fight for justice and the mission of Jesus to replicate on Earth the values of heaven, to make the world a fairer place.

The second episode was uncomfortable. At the end of our visit to Honduras, we had a meeting with Osvaldo to debrief. Tearfund said it was now reassessing its relationship with Osvaldo's development organization. There was nothing wrong with that, but then one of my colleagues added, 'In every parent-child relationship there comes a time for the young ones to grow up and take responsibility for themselves.' I could see that Osvaldo was crestfallen. On his behalf, I felt wounded. 'And in this relationship, who exactly do you think is the parent and who the child?' I asked. I was in no doubt, having spent only a few days with Osvaldo on the river and in the forest that he was the parent! If the relationship between us was not a partnership of equals, it was my brother Osvaldo who was the parent, with his lifetime of experience fighting for justice on the ground where the people of the forest lived in harmony with nature and with each other. The whole episode taught me a lesson of how unintentionally patronizing we can be. The challenge in making the world a fairer place lies in how, given the imbalance and uneven distribution of power, we proceed in true partnership with one other in our decision-making.

Tearfund and Osvaldo decided to continue their partnership.

Central America has lost 80 per cent of its forests in the past 50 years. As I write, according to *The Times*, there is 'record deforestation in Brazilian Amazon under Bolsonaro' (23 April 2020). With every tree that is lost and not replaced, the lungs of the Earth are impaired. If ever you've watched someone die of lung disease, you can imagine the consequences for the planet as we destroy our own life-support system. The defence of the deforesters is that we have already grown wealthy through our own deforestation and we shouldn't lecture others for wanting their own day in the sun.

It is true that, centuries ago, the British Isles were a heavily wooded country. There was a time when it was said that you could cross England without your feet ever touching the ground, for there were so many trees. In Bede's *Ecclesiastical History of the English People*, there's a poem by the monk Caedmon, possibly the first recorded poem in English:

Praise we the Fashioner now of Heaven's fabric,
The majesty of his might and his mind's wisdom.
Work of the world's warden, worker of all wonders,
How he the Lord of Glory everlasting,
Wrought first for the race of men Heaven as a roof tree
Then made he Middle Earth to be their mansion.

So dense was the woodland that covered the country, whenever one looked up, it was the canopy of trees that one would see. The image of heaven was not the skies, but the 'roof tree'. God was seen as 'the Fashioner' and 'the world's warden' and the earth was our 'mansion'.

In England we have, over the centuries, reduced our woodland cover to 9 per cent. In other European countries it remains between 30 and 40 per cent. When, in 2010, the Government proposed selling off the public forests, there was a huge popular outcry. Even though I was already chairing the Hillsborough Independent Panel at the time, I was also asked to chair the Independent Panel on Forestry that the Government set up to defuse the public controversy. I accepted.

The Panel was made up of representatives of all those with an interest in forests, from the National Trust to the Woodland Trust, from the Country Landowners' Association (now the Country and Land Business Association) to the Ramblers Association, from the woodland industries to wildlife charities. We agreed to travel to woodland sites in different parts of the country to meet those who were passionate about their trees. Our first visit was to the Forest of Dean. The local forester took us to a vantage point to survey a vast expanse of ancient oaks. When I made a comment about the wonders of nature, the forester corrected me, pointing out that this was not a natural landscape but a political one: 'These trees were planted to build ships for the British navy.' It was a pertinent observation. In truth, every landscape is a political one, for it reveals the values of each generation.

In the foreword to the final report of the Independent Panel on Forestry (4 July 2012), I wrote:

> Our forests and woods are nature's playground for the adventurous, museum for the curious, hospital for the stressed, cathedral for the spiritual, and a livelihood for the entrepreneur. They are a microcosm of the cycle of life in which each and every part is dependent on the other; forests and woods are the benefactor of all, purifying the air that we breathe and distilling the water of life.

This interdependence is the basis of an environmental ethic and of environmental justice. We are all beneficiaries of the trees. How, though, do we invest in trees across the planet in a way that is equitable and shares the responsibility for the well-being of our present and future generations? The ethical questions may be clear; the practical answers are complex.

When the poet Gerard Manley Hopkins lamented the felling of the Binsey poplars in 1879 to make sleepers for the construction of the Great Western Railway, he wrote:

> O if we but knew what we do
> When we delve or hew –

Hack and rack the growing green! . . .
Where we, even where we mean
To mend her we end her,
When we hew or delve . . .

Of course, today, few people would object to the Great Western Railway, not least because it has many environmental benefits, such as taking carbon-heavy traffic off the roads. The truth is that no human activity is environmentally neutral. All that we do has an impact. The issue is how to live sustainably, enjoying the fruits of God's creation today without jeopardizing the enjoyment and well-being of future generations. Trees go to the heart of intergenerational justice. The report of the Independent Panel on Forestry recommended that the forests should remain in trust for the nation and not be sold off into private hands, which have a poor record of woodland management, which is vital for the forests to flourish. Such a partnership with nature is an example of how humanity exists as a part of nature and not apart from it. Both Government and Opposition accepted this and other recommendations that have now led to an ambitious programme of tree-planting in both urban and rural settings.

One of the other discoveries I made was that, in the UK, forests and woodlands make the largest recreational provision, creating huge benefits for both our physical and mental health. People are rediscovering that woodlands are indeed a playground for the adventurous and a hospital for the stressed. And in these arboreal cathedrals, people find themselves increasingly in touch with the spiritual side of their nature.

The poet John Clare wrestled with issues of mental well-being and often walked through a valley of despair. Digging deep into the soil of nature was the antidote to his depression. He captured the healing balm of trees in his poem 'The hollow tree':

How oft a summer shower hath started me
To seek for shelter in a hollow tree.
Old huge ash-dotterel wasted to a shell
Whose vigorous head still grew and flourished well
Where ten might sit upon the battered floor
And still look round discovering room for more
And he who chose a hermit life to share
Might have a door and make a cabin there.
They seemed so like a house that our desires
Would call them so and make our gipsey fires
And eat field dinners of the juicey peas
Till we were wet and drabbled to the knees
But in our old tree-house rain as it might
Not one drop fell although it rained all night.

Trees figure prominently in the Christian story, which is set within a triangle of trees. The Bible opens with the revelation of God as the gardener who plants a garden in Eden with beautiful trees bearing food, and at the centre of which stands the tree of life. Trees are an expression of the bounty of God's providence, as the Chief Rabbi pointed out.

The second point in the triangle comes with the arrival of Jesus, the child of Adam, the Child of the Earth. This child of a carpenter, a fashioner of wood, was nailed to a tree as he took into his own body the bruising blemishes of the world before he was then laid in the heart of the Earth.

The third point of this trinity of trees appears at the end of the Bible when, in the book of Revelation, we're given a vision of a renewed and regenerated world where, in answer to the Lord's Prayer, heaven comes down to the Earth. Straddling the river of the water of life, the tree of life reappears, with its leaves for 'the healing of the nations' (Revelation 22.2). Again, long before people knew the science of trees, there was a religious intuition that they were essential to health.

Jonathon Porritt, in his book *Hope in Hell*, published in 2020 (Simon & Schuster), argues that we have just one decade left to confront the climate emergency. He sets out in detail the measures that must be taken to ensure environmental justice. Quoting Winston Churchill from another context, he presses the point: 'Owing to past neglect, in the face of the plainest warnings, we have entered upon a period of danger. The era of procrastinations, of half measure, of soothing and baffling expedients, of delays, is coming to its close. In its place we are entering a period of consequences . . . We cannot avoid this period; we are in it now' (p. 130).

Porritt pleads that the breakdown of the climate must be framed as a matter of justice, and invokes Naomi Klein's argument that every country must make sure that it actually hits the steep emission reduction targets mandated by science. Sadly, those who are bearing the brunt of the consequences of climate change through deforestation, through droughts and floods and displacement are those who have very little power to do anything about it; and those of us who are the major causes of such consequences have shown equally little will to do anything about it. In many ways, the strategy of adaptation and mitigation appears to have let us off the hook in the short term but, ultimately, there will be no escaping what is urgently needed. The Thames Barrier was erected to protect London. It was raised 4 times in the 1980s, over 35 times in the 1990s and in total it has been raised some 200 times. The increasing number of flood defence closures shows both the reality and the seriousness of climate change. And if the capital, especially Westminster and the City of London, had been flooded as many times as the Thames Barrier has been raised, it would surely have generated the will to act more urgently in concert with other nations to cut our emissions and to invest in the leaves of the trees with their unique power to heal the nations of the Earth.

I'm conscious of my own hypocrisy in flying to other parts of the world. I share these experiences to underline the need to act urgently, knowing that no amount of offsetting through tree-planting absolves the hypocrisy. In Honduras, I witnessed the devastating landslides that followed the rains because the trees were no longer there to hold the soil in place; in West Bengal, I walked through the paddy fields where young children drowned because they could not run fast enough to escape the floods that came with the super cyclones; in Kenya, I saw the treeless landscapes and the mountains of poisonous plastic bottles that brought water to the people instead of the now dried-up rivers. But in Nairobi Cathedral, I heard a note of hope. If you go into a church, you'll often hear the congregation saying the Lord's Prayer, and the congregation will often pause between 'thy will be done' and 'on earth as it is in heaven', thus abstracting God's will from the very place it is meant to be done. It has made me think that this is one of the reasons the Church has been so slow to grasp the divine imperative of acting justly on and in the Earth. So my joy overflowed when no one in the Nairobi congregation took a breath between 'thy will be done' and 'on earth as it is heaven' and prayed with one voice, 'thy will be done on earth as it is in heaven'. The earthing of heaven.

I went to India to see the development work being done by the partners of Christian Aid. I met Ardhentu Chatterjee, a development worker who shared his life with the landless men of West Bengal. They were the hopeless poor who had no prospect of improving their lot in life. They were the incarnation of poverty and the human manifestation of an unfair world. Ardhentu taught them how to cultivate the unclaimed strips of no man's land that bordered the roads. They planted a particular tree that grew two metres in twelve months. It gave food for animals and firewood to keep people warm in the cold nights. Ardhentu went from village to village, teaching others how to grow herbs for medicines, and he taught me the poetry of Rabindranath Tagore.

> This is my prayer to thee, my Lord –
> Strike, strike at the root of penury in my heart.
> Give me strength lightly to bear my joys and sorrows.
> Give me strength to make my love fruitful in service.
> Give me strength never to disown the poor or bend my
>   knees before insolent might.
> Give me strength to raise my mind high above daily
>   trifles.
> And give me strength to surrender my strength to thy
>   will with love.

Ardhentu, a Hindu, brought to life for me one of the famous parables of Jesus about a sower (not necessarily a landowner) who went out to sow seeds. Maybe Jesus had in mind the landless poor of his own day. Some of the seed fell by the wayside, rootless; some fell on the roadside rocks; some were strangled by thorns. But some of the seed hit good soil and yielded a surprising harvest. I watched the men drinking in every word that Ardhentu spoke. Beneath the wide skies of West Bengal and across a landscape mottled in greens and browns by a low-lying lazy sun, he talked as he walked and they followed him. It was like watching Jesus being followed by his own disciples hanging on his every word, hungry and thirsty for a new and fairer world.

Many writers from the Christian tradition concentrate on the Old Testament, Genesis, the Psalms and the prophets, to make the case for environmental justice. What the young people in the schools in and around Liverpool did in the millennium year was to make me ask what the New Testament, the Gospels and, in particular, Jesus had to say about the Earth. It was these discoveries that fundamentally changed my own understanding of the connection between Christianity and environmental justice.

Making similar discoveries before me were other Christians from the evangelical tradition, such as Peter Harris, the founder of A Rocha International, and, notably, two eminent scientists: the late Sir John Houghton, the atmospheric physicist and co-chair of the Intergovernmental Panel on Climate Change, and Professor R. J. (Sam) Berry, who understood the need to persuade our American cousins that the Bible teaches us to care for God's creation.

In the USA, evangelicals who take a literal interpretation of the Bible as the authority for their beliefs exercise huge political influence. The vast majority of them have been very sceptical about environmental issues. I hope they will forgive what may seem to them a caricature of their position, but they dismiss environmentalism as bad science, bad religion, bad for business and bad for America. One evangelical leader told me he saw it as a Trojan horse bringing to America a form of socialism that would bring the nation to its knees by pricing American products out of world markets and transporting American jobs to countries such as India and China. But, as in the UK, there were exceptions in the USA, such as leading evangelicals Richard Cizik and Jim Ball, who responded positively to the work of Sir John Houghton and to the scientific evidence about the changing climate that he was able to provide. Houghton was also able to show them how the Bible lays on us a moral and spiritual imperative to care for God's creation. Cizik and Ball found these arguments compelling.

During the first decade of the present millennium, a number of people who could see that caring for God's creation was a priority began to work together to see if we might be able to change the hearts and minds of evangelical leadership in America. We mounted several conferences at St George's House, in Windsor, over the years. Through Jim and Rich, we invited influential men and women of evangelical faith to come to learn from distinguished experts about how caring for God's creation is based on good science, good religion and is good for both business and America. We had large attendances at each of the gatherings.

The icing on the cake, or, rather, the gilt edge of the invitation, was the final day, when the Prince of Wales received everyone at his home in Gloucestershire to see for themselves the merits of organic farming. The conference ended with tea with His Royal Highness at Highgrove House. Prince Charles read Psalm 104 and spoke about his concerns for the planet, then went around the room asking guests what they had learnt. I cannot claim that all were converted by the conferences, but there were not a few who had their minds opened to the science and their hearts opened to the moral and spiritual imperative to care for God's world. One of the guests was Joel Hunter, pastor of Northland Church, Orlando, a megachurch with a congregation around the world of thousands. He was a spiritual adviser to President Obama and now stands out as an unequivocal advocate 'for protecting God's creation for the sake of victims of pollution-caused climate change' (<http://joelhunter.com/bio>).

The road to environmental justice is a long and winding one. Essentially, the future of the planet will be determined by America and China. The question that constantly challenges me is the one that Jesus posed at the end of the parable about the widow going in search of justice: 'When the Child of the Earth

A picture of my consecration in 1994, painted by our daughter, Harriet
(From family's collection)

Ben, five, and Sophie, three – our grandchildren
(From family's collection)

Hillsborough Independent Panel in the Lady Chapel, Liverpool
Cathedral, 12 September 2012
(REUTERS/Alamy Stock Photo)

Margaret Aspinall, Chair of the Hillsborough
Family Support Group, addressing the second
inquest, 11 May 2016

(PA Images/Alamy Stock Photo)

Anne Williams, founder of Hope for Hillsborough,
attending the Hillsborough memorial service,
15 April 2013, shortly before her death

(PA Images/Alamy Stock Photo)

A gift from the Cathedral Chapter of the poem 'Liverpool', about Hillsborough, by Carol Ann Duffy and illustrated by Stephen Raw
(Reproduced by kind permission of Carol Ann Duffy and Stephen Raw)

Montage portrait by Anthony Brown from the '100 Heads Thinking as One' exhibition to mark Liverpool as Capital of Culture in 2008
(Reproduced by kind permission of Anthony Brown)

Ardhentu Chatterjee working with
the landless, West Bengal
(From family's collection)

Nariman Gasimoglu giving his paper
on the Amazon
(Reproduced by kind permission of Nariman
Gasimoglu)

Pastor Joel Hunter (left) and Jim Ball (right) consult with Sir John
Houghton (centre) on caring for the environment
(Reproduced by kind permission of Kara Ball)

Tim Parry, killed by a bomb in Warrington's Bridge Street in 1993 and inspiration for the Tim Parry Johnathan Ball Peace Foundation

(Reproduced by kind permission of Colin and Wendy Parry)

Anthony Walker, murdered with an axe, 30 July 2005, aged 18. The inspiration for the Anthony Walker Foundation

(PA Images/Alamy Stock Photo)

Dome of the Rock, Jerusalem
(From family's collection)

Church of the Holy Sepulchre, Jerusalem,
with the guardian who offered me the key
(From family's collection)

'If you're the Bishop I'm the Pope.' Gift
from a prisoner on the occasion of a visit
to HM Prison Risley
(From family's collection)

Icon: 'I am the light of the world'
(From family's collection)

[the Son of Man] comes, will he find faith [in a God of justice] on the earth?' (Luke 18.8, my translation).

Postscript

'Thought for the Day', 18 November 2020

There's a connection and a disconnection between the new COVID vaccines and the upcoming speech by the Prime Minister ahead of chairing the next UN climate conference. The climate and the virus both threaten our existence.

But whereas the virus is beginning to meet its match, the changing climate is still rampant. The difference? We feel and fear the nearness of the virus; as to the climate, in spite of sporadic flooding and occasional droughts, it's not yet touched our nerve.

The global pandemic shows that where there's a fear, there's a way. With the climate, there seems insufficient fear to find a way. That's why we need prophets as much as they did in the Old Testament. But as many of them find, they're often without honour in their own country.

Some years ago, I spent time listening to young people's dreams and dreads about the future. It made me rethink my own attitude to the environment. What did Jesus have to say about the Earth? What were the Jewish and Muslim ethics of creation? I went to see the late rabbi Lord Jonathan Sacks. When I ventured that Jews might begin with Genesis, he stopped me.

'No, James. That's a very Christian way of reading the Bible on this subject!' 'No,' he repeated, 'we start in Deuteronomy with God's instruction to Moses that, as they entered the promised land, they were never to destroy a fruit-bearing tree.' Long before anyone knew the science of climate change, there was a religious intuition that trees were central to our ecology.

Just as I was leaving this 'masterclass', he posed a question. 'Do you know what the three most extraordinary words of Jesus were?' Here was the Chief Rabbi putting a Christian bishop on the spot about Jesus, and I didn't know the answer. He raised his eyebrows: 'But I say'. Apparently there's no evidence from that period of a rabbi saying, as Jesus did, 'You've heard it said, but I say . . .'.

Those three syllables are the words of a prophet in any generation – prepared to face the wind and walk against the storm of public opinion, and to persuade with hope rather than with fear. For the problem with fear is that it usually grips the soul once what is feared has already claimed the lives of many people.

4

Jesus

Ever since I was a young child, and in spite of not coming from an overtly religious family, the figure of Jesus featured strongly in my thoughts. Like many of my generation, the portrayal of Jesus by Tom Fleming in the 1956 BBC television mini-series *Jesus of Nazareth* informed my religious imagination. I remember being very distressed by Jesus' arrest, trial and crucifixion and distraught at how unfair it all was. At the same time, through my father's army posting, we moved from Wales to Scotland. The vicar of the church where my brother and I sang in the choir asked us if we would like to choose a hymn on our last Sunday. I chose 'Thou didst leave thy throne and thy kingly crown when thou camest to earth for me', with the lilting chorus: 'O come to my heart, Lord Jesus, there is room in my heart for Thee.' Ever since that day, I have sought to find room in my soul for him.

In 1959, my parents were posted to Singapore and I joined my elder brother at boarding school in Dover at the Duke of York's Royal Military School. Founded for the orphans of the Napoleonic Wars, its original building still stands in Chelsea. It was very spartan. We wore battledress for our uniform and marched to meals to the sound of a military band.

I came under the influence of the chaplain and his wife, Clifford and Nora Davies, whose open home was a refuge for me. I sang in the chapel choir and served at the altar. On Saturdays, after the evening meal, which was always a pretty raucous affair with the results of games against other schools announced to great cheers, there was always a film, which was compulsory. One night, it failed to show and we had real free time! I felt led to go to the chapel, which was situated on the edge of the playing fields. I walked the length of the carpeted aisle and knelt down at the altar rail. Every Sunday, we heard stirring sermons by preachers from all over the Commonwealth who had come to study at St Augustine's College, Canterbury. Their messages were often about the tough conditions back home, but they were always consistent in their uncomplaining testimony as to how alive Jesus was to them.

As I knelt, I began to weep teenage tears, asking Christ to forgive me and to guide me into the future. The prayer was a form of the Jesus Prayer, as yet unknown to me and so central to Orthodox spirituality: 'Lord Jesus Christ, Son of God, have mercy on me a sinner.' I asked God to show me what he wanted me to do with my life. The prayer was framed by both the limitations and the expectations of an adolescent mind, but it was real. It brought with it an in-flooding wave of peace and joy. I wept again. I wanted to dance across the playing fields back to my boarding house, but that was not the sort of thing to be seen doing in a boys' military boarding school!

It was not until my twenties that I discovered an elderly widowed great-aunt had prayed for me every day of my life since my baptism as a baby. Mary Wise was a Welsh poet who lived into her nineties and worshipped at Brecon Cathedral, where at the altar rail she once had a vision of Jesus. The amethyst from her necklace forms the heart of my bishop's ring.

These youthful spiritual experiences brought with them a simple longing to look out for those in need and always to be fair. I recall that when I became head boy (or chief school prefect), I would frequently challenge my own judgement, asking myself whether or not I was being fair. In spite of my many failures, that has remained me with me all my life. From time to time, I still think back to those scenes in *Jesus of Nazareth*, to the betrayal and the brutality that lay in store for Jesus, even though he was innocent and good. I wanted to dive through the screen and into the scene and scream, 'Don't do it!' It was the manifest injustice that seared my soul.

In the face of injustice, Jesus was unashamed to reveal his own inner turmoil. 'My soul is troubled,' he confessed to his friends as he contemplated his destiny of betrayal, false arrest, trumped-up charges, wrongful conviction and execution. In Greek, 'My soul is shipwrecked.' Emotionally and spiritually, he was on the rocks. Shattered by despair, we can either retreat deeper into ourselves and become more isolated or reach out to others as we come to the end of our selves. Jesus found solace in his friendship with Lazarus and his two sisters, Martha and Mary. The latter took expensive perfume to refresh his feet, which she then dried with the tresses of her hair. Judas complained about squandering good money, earning a stern rebuke from Jesus: 'Leave her alone' (John 12.7). Whatever physical, emotional or spiritual comfort came to him in his hour of need, his shipwrecked soul was being succoured. Like countless people encountering a travesty of justice, Jesus found solace in a community. This episode exposes his vulnerability and humanity. In spite of his charisma and natural authority, he was a genuine human being with love to give and the need to be loved. I suspect that this side of his character added to his appeal and popularity. Crowds got up early to listen to him. They flocked to him on the shores of the Sea of Galilee or in the Temple in Jerusalem. They loved his ideas. They were enthralled by his stories. They knew he was there for them, on their side and on the side of justice.

Living in an occupied country, they longed for the day when the foreign power would be overthrown. Some even thought that Jesus would be the one to lead the rebellion. The various authorities, civic and religious, were wary of Jesus' popularity in such an unstable country, but the people who had the biggest problem with Jesus were the 'Church' of his day, especially its leaders. You'd have thought that a man preaching love and telling others to be selfless would have been welcomed with open arms by faith leaders. Not so! They loathed him. Jesus hammered home the two great commandments, to love God and to love your neighbour as yourself, but he also fearlessly exposed the hypocrisy of much of their religion. He accused them of betraying both their faith and the people in favour of indulging in all the prissy practices of their religion. They, in turn, felt insulted. They longed to be rid of him. The story of the tension between Jesus and the religious leaders is an object lesson in the danger of organized religion. The charge that Jesus levelled against the religious leaders was a serious indictment: 'You . . . neglect justice [or judgement] and the love of God' (Luke 11.42).

The fact that Jesus talked about both the judgement of God and the love of God in the same breath presents a challenge to the liberal-minded today. We can cheer Jesus' condemnation of religious hypocrisy, but we find the idea of harnessing God's love to the notion of divine judgement much more difficult to digest.

In my study, over the fireplace, hangs an icon of Jesus. On a gold background and crowned with a halo, Christ stares out into the room, holding a Bible open at a page that says in Greek, the language of the New Testament, 'I am the light of the world. Whoever follows me will never walk in darkness but will have the light of life' (John 8.12). I asked our little grandson, three at the time, if he liked my new picture of Jesus. 'No', he replied emphatically. 'He looks cross.' And so he does! Ben, unaware of the niceties of understanding icons, was unafraid to speak his mind about how he saw the character of Christ. In fact, there were times in the life of Jesus when he was cross, rightly furious. It was precisely because he was motivated by love that he got so angry at those things and those people who diminished others. Righteous anger is an expression of love. That may come as a surprise to us, but not to Jesus, who set his face against oppression and injustice. At the heart of love lies an imperative to act against injustice, especially on behalf of victims who do not have the power to resist the oppression. Jesus often showed righteous indignation at the way people were being treated.

When his own followers tried to shoo children away for wasting Jesus' time, he got angry. When Judas sought to stop Mary anointing his feet with expensive perfume in his hour of need, Jesus got angry. When he heard that Herod had killed his cousin and wanted to kill him too, he got angry calling him 'a fox'. When the religious leaders took advantage of ordinary people and bamboozled them with endless rituals, he got angry and swore at them, calling them 'fools' and 'hypocrites'.

There was nothing meek or mild about Jesus condemning those who intimidated ordinary people. Just as you would expect a parent, teacher or carer to act against bullying, so love must move against any force that belittles or destroys another person.

One Sabbath day, Jesus was confronted by a woman with mental and physical health issues. He called her over, laid hands on her and healed her. She was ecstatic! The man in charge at the synagogue was livid. Why? Because Jesus had made the woman well on the day of rest, in effect working on the Sabbath. It was Jesus' turn to be livid! 'You can untie and water an animal on the Sabbath, but you can't free a human being from their prison!' Jesus had one excoriating word for the religious leader: 'Hypocrite!', And then he got even tougher. Invoking a stronger word packed with a moral punch, he challenged him, 'Did it not behove us [was it not morally necessary], to release this woman from such an evil grip that had held her for so long, for eighteen years?' (Luke 13.16, my translation).

For Jesus, this wasn't just a matter of healing the sick and comforting the broken-hearted. There was a moral imperative to setting this woman free. And anybody who didn't see that, or anyone who, God forbid, resisted her liberation was guilty of an injustice even if, *especially* if, he or she was a religious leader.

The little word that Jesus used, meaning 'it is necessary' or 'it behoves', is found on his lips many times in Luke's account of his life. A couple of chapters earlier, he was laying it on the line, saying, 'It is necessary for you to act upon and not overlook the justice and love of God' (Luke 11:42, my translation). The seeking of justice was one of the moral imperatives that motivated him and ruled his life. I grew up thinking that the personal relationship with Jesus was the priority of the Christian faith and the call to do justice was a consequence of belief. However, the tenor of Jesus' teaching and actions shows that doing justice was, for him, an equally important imperative. Indeed, how could a person be close to Jesus and enter into a personal relationship with God, the God of justice and mercy, without at the same time being caught up in the divine dynamic of '[doing] justice, [loving] kindness, and [walking] humbly with . . . God' (Micah 6.8)? Personal faith and social justice are two inseparable sides of the one coin of Christianity. There is no life in a faith without action.

The first time that Jesus was recorded using this ethical phrase 'it is necessary' or 'it behoves' was when he was a teenager. He and his family had been in Jerusalem visiting the Temple for an annual festival. When they began their journey home with their relatives, unbeknown to his parents, Jesus had stayed behind to carry on questioning the Temple teachers. He showed remarkable understanding and insight for a twelve-year-old. When his parents realized that he was not with them, they returned to the Temple and chided him for going missing and giving them so much grief. The way Jesus answered his parents showed self-awareness unusual for his age, asking, 'Why did you search for me? Did you not know that in the things of my father it is necessary to be me?' (Luke 2.49, my translation) Although his parents hadn't a clue what he was talking about, Jesus was pleading with them to respect him and his identity. To be true to himself was, for Jesus, not just a matter of personal preference. It was a moral and spiritual necessity. Like all adolescents, Jesus was in transition. He was growing up. Either side of this contretemps with his parents, we are told that, 'The child grew and became strong, filled with wisdom; and the favour of God was upon him' and, 'Jesus increased in wisdom and in years, and in divine and human favour' (Luke 2.40, 52). These sentences describe Jesus' physical, intellectual, spiritual and social development.

The meaning of the word for 'growing up' in Greek, the language of the New Testament, comes from the idea of chopping away obstacles. Human growth, which goes on for the whole of life, is about negotiating our way through a series of crises. Adolescence is but a taste of what is to come! It is through these struggles that our personality emerges and is shaped, and that our identity becomes known to our self. It's in adolescence that there can be tension between parents and their children, especially when the latter no longer conform to the ambitions of the former.

'Did you not know that in the things of my father it is necessary to be me?' are the first recorded words of Jesus. They laid the foundations of his self-understanding and set the course of his life. 'The things of [his] father' encompassed God's will for his life. We are never too young (or too old) to consider God's call on our life, but what impresses me most about the exchange between Jesus and his mother is the unassailable necessity of

69

being allowed to find and express his own identity and his own purpose in life even at the age of twelve. In other words, identity and purpose are not optional extras to his or our existence; they were and are integral to our being. I know this is a leap of faith, but it is not unreasonable to believe that there is a moral necessity for every human being to know who he or she is.

Families, parents, peer groups, schools, friends, social and mainstream media, as well as society, can all conspire to make us conform, against our truest instincts. But in the end, deep down, there's a voice in our soul, silenced maybe for a time but that grows ever louder, which says, 'I am who I am'. To echo St Paul, writing some years after Jesus' death and resurrection, 'by the grace of God I am what I am' (1 Corinthians 15.10). My identity is God's gift to me. In a just world, all people should be free to be themselves.

This immediately poses a problem. Anyone even loosely acquainted with his or her own nature, let alone human nature generally, will be aware of the gap between what we are and what we ought to be. Countless times, we fall short in what we think, say and do. In our worst and most honest moments, we would readily confess to there being a chasm between the 'ideal me' and 'the real me', and conclude, in the words of the Book of Common Prayer, 'There is no health in us.' How then, can we expect to be allowed to be ourselves when our selves are so flawed?

If we fast-forward through Luke's account of the life of Jesus, we come across his encounter with a man called Zacchaeus. He collected taxes from the people on behalf of the occupying Romans. He was corrupt. He overcharged the people and pocketed the profits. Tax collectors were generally hated as crooks and collaborators. Zacchaeus was a chief tax collector in the town of Jericho and, therefore, was rich. He was the opposite of Jesus, who by then was an itinerant preacher living a hand-to-mouth existence and dependent on other people's hospitality and generosity. Opposites attract. There was something about Jesus that intrigued Zacchaeus, who went to extraordinary lengths to catch sight of him. A small man, he climbed a tree to see over the crowd. There was something about that little rich man huddled up a tree that stopped Jesus in his tracks. Having previously been at a dinner with a crowd of tax officials, he knew his name (a chief tax collector would be famous as well as infamous). He called out, 'Zacchaeus, hurry and come down; for I must stay at your house today' (Luke 19.5).

It is difficult to exaggerate how loathsome Zacchaeus was in the eyes of the people. We need to understand what a social leper he was in order to appreciate fully the enormity of what Jesus did and said to him. He didn't just invite himself into the crooked man's home, thus risking alienating the poor, who loved him and hated the tax collectors; Jesus also said something even more arresting: I paraphrase, 'For today it is *necessary* for me (it behoves me) to stay in your house.' That word, 'necessary', which Jesus used to underline the imperative to practise the love and the justice of God, is the very word he used to justify his coming to the home of the vile Zacchaeus. As Zacchaeus fell out of the branches and scurried into his house followed by Jesus, a message went out to the world that no one, however wicked, was beyond the pale of God's coming and there were no limits to God's love. God was without prejudice and without boundaries. God's commitment to justice walked hand in hand with a moral purpose to be merciful and to embrace and rescue sinners.

The impact on Zacchaeus was immense and legendary. The coming of Jesus into his life was transformative. Zacchaeus welcomed him with joy. What must it be like to be universally hated and then to discover that someone who is greatly loved by the people wants to be with *you*? Larger than life, although small in stature, Zacchaeus and his story begin to answer the question of how we can reconcile our identity with the reality of our flawed nature. How can we live, being true to ourselves, while at the same time owning up to the truth about our short-comings? The turning point for Zacchaeus was hearing Jesus speak his name. His longing to see who Jesus was showed that, although he was successful and rich, there was a spiritual curiosity that had yet to be satisfied.

This yearning curiosity centred on a man who was popular with the poor and preached fearlessly about the love and justice of God. I imagine that Zacchaeus was shocked to hear Jesus call his name. He welcomed him into his home with open arms – 'joyfully'. What he discovered through this encounter is that whatever he had done wrong, in accumulating his wealth and in the way he had treated the poor and defrauded the people, these deeds did not, of themselves, create an impossible barrier between him and Jesus, the champion of those he cheated. This didn't please the crowd, who would have hanged Zacchaeus there and then from the sycamore tree, but Jesus represented a different kind of justice, one blended with mercy. Or even a justice preceded by mercy.

Out of love for all humanity, Jesus was gripped by a necessity to enter Zacchaeus' home, his household and his life, and 'to stay'. Those in the crowd were entitled to grumble. After all that Zacchaeus had done, he didn't deserve any visit from a messenger of God, an advocate of the oppressed who had made it his mission 'to bring good news to the poor'. Yet Jesus knew that there were other forms of poverty. You could be financially rich but, through your own selfishness, be morally and spiritually bankrupt. What Zacchaeus discovered, as he sought to see him, was that Jesus represented a God who was 'slow to anger, and of great mercy' (Psalm 145.8, KJV) and did not deal with us according to what we deserved. Thank God!

Jesus met Zacchaeus on his own turf and accepted him as he was. He respected his identity without condoning his injustices, just as he honours our own personality without endorsing our vices. He followed Zacchaeus to his home, but saw that he was lost. It was Jesus' moral purpose to go in search of him and all the lost.

The encounter was life-changing, the impact enormous. Zacchaeus responded positively to Jesus' presence in his life. Having tasted mercy, he set about righting his wrongs and doing, at last, what was just, especially to those he had defrauded. Half his wealth he gave to the poor and he gave back to those he had cheated four times what he owed them. Here was the power of mercy to induce justice. Jesus turned on its head the human approach, which seeks justice first and mercy second. Little wonder that he declared, 'Today salvation has come to this house'!

But what this episode also shows is that the creation of a more just society is achieved not simply by overhauling unjust structures but also by the internal and moral transformation of individuals. This is what William Wilberforce saw so clearly. It is a story for our times. Where there is such an uneven and unfair share of the Earth's wealth, where often the more you care for people the less you earn, the call to act justly and to love mercy should make every individual reassess the portfolio of his or her possessions. Should anyone be left thinking that this is a dutiful and joyless exercise, there's no disguising the note of joy running through the second half of the story of Zacchaeus.

The blessing that mercy and justice brought into the life of Zacchaeus mirrored the happiness to be found in another story that Jesus told about a father of two sons. The younger one asked for his share of the inheritance while their father was still alive. Even though this was tantamount to wishing his father dead, the disastrous request was granted. He squandered the lot and became destitute.

The elder son was dutiful and stood loyally by his father. The father never gave up hoping that his younger son would one day return home. And he did. Eating humble pie, he begged to be taken back – not as an heir, which he had forfeited, but as a hired hand. The father, who had been waiting for him, would have none of it. He ran to him, hugged him and kissed him. He threw a party and killed the fatted calf. The elder brother was furious and refused to join the celebration. He had slaved all his life on the estate and never asked for a penny. He could not bear his father's generosity towards his profligate brother. It all seemed so unfair. The father acknowledged his faithfulness and promised he would be the beneficiary of his estate. And the parable ends without us knowing if the elder brother ever went into the party.

I suppose the fair and just response to the child's homecoming would have been to send him packing: 'You made your bed, now lie in it.' Or: 'You wished me dead, now reap what you've sown.' Or: 'You've no one to blame but yourself.' That would have been his just desserts and exactly what his brother wanted.

However, as with Zacchaeus, mercy preceded justice, symbolized by the image of the endlessly waiting father scanning the horizon for signs of his son's homecoming. Yet justice remained intact for the elder son, for he was assured of his fair share of the estate. Explaining the father's compassion towards his younger son and the reason for the celebration, Jesus put into the father's mouth that all-important word, 'necessary': 'It was necessary to be merry and joyful' (Luke 15.32, my translation). There was a moral obligation to mark with delight and happiness that the one who had been so lost in a pit of self-destruction was now alive and home again.

Even though the brother couldn't see it, in the same way that the onlookers in Jericho resented the befriending of Zacchaeus, nevertheless Jesus was following a divine imperative to show mercy and to save the lost from themselves. The joy that marks these two scenes is an echo of an eternal sound heard in heaven whenever anyone surrenders to the mercy of God. God's justice and mercy are merrily restorative.

Although there is undoubtedly a fault-line of injustice and sorrow running through the terrain of human history, there is a greater arc of joy spanning it, of which the boldest colours are both mercy and justice. But in the temporary mire of human sadness, it is easy to lose sight of the joy 'that [is] set before' us (Hebrews 12.2).

Dostoevsky, in his novel *The Brothers Karamazov*, ponders the significance of the first miracle that Jesus did at a wedding, when he turned water into wine. 'I love that passage: It's Cana of Galilee, the first miracle . . . Ah, that miracle! Ah, that sweet miracle! It was not men's grief but their joy Christ visited, He worked His first miracle to help men's gladness.'

When I was a curate, my wife and I used to run discussion groups looking at questions of faith. It was a six-week course called Christian Basics. At the beginning of each series, people would volunteer their reasons for coming. On one occasion, after several contributions, where the reasons given for attendance were quite downbeat, a young man piped up, 'I don't connect with any of this,' he protested, 'I'm about to get married to a beautiful woman, I have a great job, I think life is wonderful – I just want to know who I have got to thank for everything!'

Christians seem to relate best to the world in its misery, but we seem to have little to say to those who are so positive about life. When our eldest daughter was eleven and starting secondary school, she was given a Gideon Bible. She came home and went up to her room. After some time she came down for tea. She had been reading the verses that are suggested for different and particularly difficult stages of life. 'Daddy,' she asked wistfully, 'is there nothing in the Bible for when you're happy?' We sometimes forget that the life of Jesus begins and ends in joy. The angels announced his birth, bringing 'tidings of great joy' (Luke 2.10, KJV). Then, later, Jesus promised his disciples that their 'sorrow shall be turned into joy' and that 'your joy may be full' (John 16.20, 24, KJV). Finally, at the end of his life, when the disciples became convinced that Jesus had risen from the dead, they went back to Jerusalem, the scene of his unfair trial and unjust death, and did so 'with great joy'.

The restoration of a just world through the mercy of God is to be celebrated with joy. Justice is the path to well-being, to peace, to harmony, to shalom (wholeness) – yes, and to joy. The father of the prodigal and sulking adult children speaks for the good Father of all, who pines for and plans the renewal of creation, declaring that there is a divine necessity to the joy and merriment in heaven when all that is apparently lost in this world is found, and all those who are spiritually lifeless come alive again.

It was early in his short-lived career that Jesus set out his stall in his home town of Nazareth. It was like a manifesto on justice. He quoted from the Hebrew Scriptures and the prophet Isaiah.

'The Spirit of the Lord is upon me,
because he has anointed me
to bring good news to the poor.
He has sent me to proclaim release to the captives
and recovery of sight to the blind,
to let the oppressed go free,
to proclaim the year of the Lord's favour.'
And he rolled up the scroll, gave it back to the attendant,
and sat down. The eyes of all in the synagogue were fixed
on him. Then he began to say to them, 'Today this scripture
has been fulfilled in your hearing.'
(Luke 4.18–21)

Like every Jewish person, Jesus was steeped in the writings of the prophets, in the Law of Moses and in the poetry of the Psalms. Here in Nazareth, in front of all the people who knew him from his youth, he spoke with the same self-awareness that had impressed the Temple teachers.

He spoke openly about the necessity of him fulfilling the prophecies of these Scriptures. At the end of his Gospel, Luke records Jesus saying explicitly, 'It is necessary that everything written about me in the Law of Moses, the Prophets and the Psalms should be fulfilled' (Luke 24.46, my translation). The Law of Moses set out the principles for establishing a just society, the prophets made their pleas in the name of the God of justice to obey those laws, and the Psalms gave the people prayers to confess when they failed or to sustain them as they fell victim to injustice and longed to live in a fairer world.

And here in Nazareth, quoting the prophet Isaiah, Jesus showed his own attitude to the injustices experienced by the poor, the prisoner, the blind, the oppressed and all those who were powerless to escape the unfair hand that fate had dealt them. The principal means at Jesus' disposal to address the misfortune of all these people was his power to heal. He did not have access to structural power that could change their conditions, but he did possess the charisma to heal them from physical and psychological trauma. He healed the physically ill whose disabilities prevented them from working, and so helped take them out of poverty.

He healed the lepers, whose contagious skin disease forced them into colonies outside the towns, and so released them from the prison of social exclusion, allowing them to rejoin society; he healed the visually impaired and set them free from discrimination; he healed those oppressed by emotional and spiritual trauma, restoring them to their right mind and mental well-being. All of this was 'good news' to those who were socially excluded.

The power that Jesus had to heal was his way of righting the wrongs that they were suffering. These interventions were not saying that, from now on, no follower of his would ever fall ill. They amounted to putting down markers for all who might think that disease and death were the last words on human existence in such an unfair world. His interventions on the part of God were a way of declaring that a new world was on its way, where injustices would be a thing of the past and justice and mercy would joyfully be the pillars of a new society.

Interestingly, the popular saying 'God is love' is never heard on the lips of Jesus. It never appears in the Gospels. In fact, it occurs just twice in the whole Bible, and then only in the letters of John. Yet the mission of Jesus is full of stories and statements about how God loves the world, sometimes in the most surprising ways.

Postscript

'Thought for the Day', Good Friday, 10 April 2020

On *Desert Island Discs* last month, Daniel Radcliffe chose a song by Nick Cave, 'Into my arms'. A love song, it begins with the sonorous line, 'I don't believe in an interventionist God but I know, darling, that you do'. That division of belief goes to the heart of the spiritual response to our current crisis of health and wealth.

Some feel there's no point to asking God for help: 'What will be will be'. Others will be on our knees begging God to protect our loved ones and to vanquish the virus. The Christian faith was born out of a belief in an interventionist God – that the one who made the world would rescue it out of the mire of so much that was now bad.

Although today – Good Friday – feeds this belief, it also fuels disbelief. The cry of Jesus from the cross, 'My God, why have you forsaken me?' looks like evidence for those who doubt that God has either the will or the power to intervene. If he couldn't rescue his own child, what hope is there for us?

Later on in Nick Cave's song, he concedes, 'But I believe in love and I know that you do, too'.

Beneath any arguments about whether or not God intervenes, there seems to be a universal conviction about the primacy of love. It's shared by people of all faiths and of none. Kind signs of it are now spreading to surprising places like seeds in the wind blown by the storm of the virus.

Like many people, I've prayed to God in difficult times. Last summer our six-year-old grandson had a tumour removed from his brain and is now undergoing twelve months of therapy. And, yes, we are praying for God to intervene. At such a time, philosophical arguments evaporate in the heat of love – love for him, for his family and in the hope that God too loves him with all his heart. That's the love we cling to in such a crisis. It's the same love that energized the life of Jesus.

At the end of Good Friday, after the questioning and the thirsting, after the giving and forgiving, after the promise of paradise and the struggling for breath, and just before he declared that it was 'finished', Jesus sighed, 'Into your hands I commend my spirit.' Into your arms.

It was his last testament to love, which in our present crisis is our best hope.

5

Suffering

'Life's so unfair!' The cry greets the news that, for example, a good person has died so young. There's never any correlation between the quality of a person's character and the quantity of suffering endured. There seems little justice when bad people sail through life and good people endure terrible afflictions. Yet, suffering is the normal human experience that affects us all – whether that be mentally, physically, emotionally or spiritually, or, in some lives, in all four ways.

Some of us seem to suffer more than others. It seems to prove that we live in a manifestly unfair world. 'For sufferance is the badge of all our tribe': so Shakespeare spoke through Shylock in *The Merchant of Venice*.

Until I was in my early thirties, I had taken pride in being a healthy person. The thought of going into hospital had filled me with dread since I was a child. Then, shortly after becoming a priest and while we were expecting our second child, I had my appendix out. There were post-op complications and I returned to hospital with a pulmonary embolism. Ten years later, at my medical to become the Bishop of Hull, I was diagnosed with type 2 diabetes, and since then have had carotid surgery, triple heart bypass surgery, removal of my gall bladder, a pacemaker fitted and a mild form of skin cancer. I have been the beneficiary of the miracle of modern medicine and have got through these various episodes with the love of Sarah and our three daughters and with the unfailing help of close colleagues and friends.

Although I bear testimony to the exceptional care of doctors and nurses, I have to confess that I was not immune to the self-pitying cry, 'Why me?' The spell spent in hospital for the pulmonary embolism punctured my faith. They used to change my blood-thinning syringe in the early hours of the morning. After one procedure, I noticed air-bubbles in the syringe and knew enough to be concerned. I asked if it could be changed. The hard-pressed nurse flicked the syringe and the air dissipated into a myriad of tiny bubbles. 'It takes a syringe full to kill you! Now go to sleep.' I lay there sweating as the minute pockets of air marched down the transparent tube towards my vein. I called the nurse again. Out of the vulnerability that all patients feel, fearing that complaining might put them on the wrong side of the nurse, I apologized for being worried, acknowledged how busy she was and pleaded for her to change the drip. She did, but with little grace, as she advised me that, in the old days, they used thick rubber tubes you couldn't see through!

When set against all the world's suffering shown on our screens, I was lucky to be where I was and getting such excellent medical care. But when you are sleepless in the early hours of the morning, it is difficult to abstract yourself from your tiny cell of fear and to moderate your own anxiety by considering other people's misfortunes. I also felt a failure. Recently ordained a priest, I was acutely aware that I felt nothing of God. I had no sense of his presence penetrating the darkness. My soul was numb, as if some epidural had anaesthetized my inner being. I tried to pray, but every thought evaporated as soon as it came into my head.

Some time later, while convalescing at home, I was walking past the school at the end of our road. I could hear children playing behind the tall stone wall. Their shouting and their laughter lifted my spirits. I then heard a child crying and a teacher trying to console her. I was stopped in my tracks when I realized that the distressed child was my own daughter. Part of me wanted to leap over the wall, take her in my arms and tell her, 'Daddy's here. You'll be all right. Don't worry. I'm here', but another part of me knew that I could do no such thing. If every time she got hurt I catapulted myself into her life, how would she ever learn to trust other people or discover resources within herself to handle life's obstacles or grow in self-confidence or even trust God? With a heavy heart, I walked on by. Did I love her less? No. I loved her more, in spite of the wall that divided us and separated me from her and her distress. This episode later gave me cause to think that those dark nights in hospital, when God seemed so silent and distant and when everything seemed so unfair, were not the days of loveless abandonment that I felt so acutely at the time.

For people of faith, the example of Jesus' suffering can be consoling. He, too, knew the serendipity of life's unfairness. He was among that company of good people who died young. His trial was unfair, his death unjust. In spite of all his explanations, his disciples found his suffering incomprehensible. How could God let such a good person suffer?

Jesus was candid about the inevitability of his own painful destiny. He knew that the people whom he championed would one day turn against him as he failed to fulfil their earth-bound expectations. In spite of his popularity, he had a premonition that he would be rejected, not just by those in authority but also by the people themselves. But there was another dimension to his fate. He believed that there was a *necessity* to his own suffering. Half the sayings that begin with him saying 'It is necessary' relate to his destiny and to his suffering.

'It is necessary for the Son of Man to suffer many things and to be rejected by the elders . . . and be killed' (Luke 9.22); 'It is necessary to journey on because it's not possible for a prophet to die outside Jerusalem' (Luke 13.33); 'It is necessary for those things written about me to be fulfilled . . . he was reckoned with transgressors' (Luke 22.37); 'It is necessary for the Son of Man to be delivered into the hands of sinful people to be crucified and to rise again on the third day' (Luke 24.7, my translations).

Why should it have been 'necessary' for Jesus to suffer? Was it because, in such a manifestly unjust world, God the Maker felt a responsibility to identify as closely as possible with those whom he had created in his image and who had become victims of injustice? Whatever the origin of evil and sin, did God the Maker, out of love for what he had made, want to be completely at one with us? In the cruel world in which Jesus lived, most people had every right to believe that God had abandoned them. Disease and death seemed to be the last word on human existence.

They could have been forgiven for thinking that God was indifferent to the indignities and injustices inflicted on them by the occupying power. To counter this hopelessness, Jesus pointed to the natural world to prove God's providence and presence in their lives. As we read in Matthew 6.28–30:

> Consider the lilies of the field, how they grow; they neither toil nor spin, yet I tell you, even Solomon in all his glory was not clothed like one of these. But if God so clothes the grass of the field, which is alive today and tomorrow thrown into the oven, will he not much more clothe you – you of little faith?

Later, pointing from the earth to the sky, beyond the flowers to the birds, he said, 'Are not two sparrows sold for a penny? Yet not one of them will fall to the ground apart from your Father. And even the hairs of your head are all counted. So do not be afraid; you are of more value than many sparrows' (Matthew 10.29–31). Jesus conjures up a picture of an injured sparrow, fallen from the sky and cradled on the ground by the Creator, such is God's presence in and with the whole of his wounded creation.

Tim Parry was a twelve-year-old boy who was murdered by the IRA. They detonated a bomb in Warrington in March 1993. His father, Colin, wrote about his dying in *Tim: An ordinary boy* (Hodder & Stoughton, 1995):

> I had decided that I would ask the nursing staff to move all the tubes attached to Tim to the far side of the bed and then move him over from the centre of the bed to the far side. This would give me space to lie down on the near side of the bed next to Tim and to hold him closely, as I had so desperately wanted to do all that week.

> ... I removed my leather jacket and gently got on to the bed and lay down next to our son. For the first time since early Saturday morning I was able to make proper contact with him, and I put my left arm across his chest with the fingers of my left hand around the upper part of his right arm. I put my lips to his swollen cheek and kissed him many times. I then kissed him many more times on his lips. While I was so close to him, I bade Tim my lasting and loving farewells. As I did so, I sobbed openly, with every fibre of my body aching agonisingly for this son of ours to rest in peace free from pain for all eternity. I told him I did not know what I was going to do without him, that the gap he would leave in his family's life would be huge and yawning.

> After perhaps five minutes, Nurse Colfer knocked gently on the door, opened it slightly and asked if they could come back into the room. I asked for a few moments more to recover my composure.

Getting off the bed was agonising because I knew this was to be the last time I would hold my son properly, until the next life.

This episode of a father's love for his dying child, 'with every fibre of [his]body aching agonisingly', opened my eyes to the bond between the one who loves and the beloved in a time of adversity. The intensity of that love sounds like a bow drawn slowly across a tightly wound string, both painful and beautiful. Without demeaning this last act of love by calling it an analogy, I began to see in Colin's grieving intimacy with Tim an intimation of how God is with us in our own suffering.

Such a comparison does not mitigate the force of Colin and Wendy's objection: 'How could life be so terribly cruel and unjust?' And even when we look at their pain through the experience of the crucifixion of Jesus, we find that his own brutal death does not answer their question; it amplifies it. As the question gets louder with every injustice, it brings under scrutiny the very nature of God himself.

What Jesus began to show us was that God is never a distant spectator of our suffering. Whatever has happened to the world and however it has happened, the pain has afflicted God. Even beyond the boundaries of space and time that define the limits of our earthly existence, God was and is and will forever be conscious of, and affected by, those forces of darkness that are threatened by light.

In the very last book in the Bible, there's a hint that the reality of suffering and sacrifice predates the foundation of the world. The visionary in the book of Revelation describes a vision of Jesus in heaven as 'the Lamb that was slain before the foundation of the world' (Revelation 13.8, my translation). Poetically, it implies that the merciless killing of Jesus in a particular place and time was already known in the landscape of eternity.

It suggests that evil and sin, which became manifest with the creating of humanity, were already exercising the heart of God before the foundation of the world. So when Jesus came and revealed himself in fulfilment of a prophecy as 'a man of sorrows and acquainted with grief' (Isaiah 53.3, my translation), he was displaying characteristics not just of his earthly existence but also of his heavenly and eternal being.

As I've wrestled with these ideas, I'm conscious that they are very abstract, and so what follows are two images that seek to humanize these concepts. The first tells of God's intimate acquaintance with sorrow and grief; the second explores how God incorporates all that we endure, as both agents and victims of suffering and injustice, into his overall purpose without diminishing either his love or our freedom.

In a devastating earthquake, a school collapsed, killing all but one of the children and all the teachers. The child was rescued from the rubble still alive. He was rushed to the hospital, where an emergency team of doctors and nurses laboured for hours to save his life while his mother waited outside, hoping for a miracle.

After hours of painstaking surgery, the team failed and the little boy died. The surgeon then took it on himself to break the terrible news to the child's mother. She broke down, became hysterical and lunged at the surgeon, pummeling his chest and screaming, 'No, no, no!' Instead of pushing her away, he held her tighter to himself until her sobbing subsided and she rested cradled in his arms. At that moment, tears welled up in his own eyes and trickled down his face. He had come to the hospital immediately after he had heard that his own child had been killed in the earthquake. Like the surgeon, our own Father in heaven feels the pain of loss. God the Father was bereft of his own child as surely as Mary, his mother, was bereft of Jesus. All three persons of the Trinity are acquainted with grief.

The second image is one that I return to when I find it difficult to reconcile the injustices of the world with a belief in God as a loving and powerful force. I imagine a master painter at work at his easel. He creates on his canvas with oils the vision of his mind's eye. As he does so, he is surrounded by beautiful but mischievous grandchildren, who all have their own designs on the painting, dipping their fingers in the palette of paints and daubing the canvas. So creative a painter is he, and so infinitely patient is he as a grandfather, that instead of scolding his charges and shooing them away, he embraces and incorporates every single smudge, integrating them into his own design so that they add depth, relief, texture and luminosity to the vision of his mind and heart that he is realizing with oils on the canvas.

So God, in his patient love for us, slow to anger and abounding in mercy, does not destroy us as we bruise his world, but continually works with the material that we abuse so as to redeem his creation to an even greater degree of glory. God not only sustains all that he has made and makes but he also restores, augments, enlarges and glorifies it, thus holding in perfect tension his sovereign love and our willful freedom.

The fact that God is with us and shares in our suffering, the fact that God is often silent when we suffer, and the fact that we hope there might be some grander design at work in that silence: these facts do not mitigate the severe testing of our resilience in the face of so many injustices.

The parable of Jesus that I associate so much with Hillsborough opens with Jesus explaining 'their need to pray always and not to lose heart' (Luke 18.1). Jesus knew that, faced with all the injustice in this life, the temptation to throw in the towel was very real and strong. Praying was his antidote to giving up. But the praying was not about meekly giving in and surrendering to life's injustices. It was about persistently pressing forwards for justice to be done. Those who look to Jesus and pray for God's kingdom to come and for his 'will to be done on earth as it is in heaven' are setting their face against the suffering inflicted by injustice. Florence Nightingale, Williams Wilberforce, Josephine Butler, Lord Shaftesbury, Oscar Romero, Martin Luther King, Jr, and Mother Theresa are famous figures from the past who prayed and fought against injustice and refused to give up the fight.

Also, unknown and unsung, yet equally effective in the earthing of heaven, there are those simple acts of resistance by ordinary people who, in their daily lives, challenge unfairness wherever they see it, especially on behalf of others and pledge always to be fair in their own dealings, even when it is to their own disadvantage, and so make the world a fairer place. That's how justice overcomes injustice.

These are the instruments and the signs of a new world that is coming, where injustice and suffering, disease and death will no longer be the last words on human existence. They are the prelude to that new Jerusalem where God will declare: 'I am making all things new' (Revelation 21.5), while at the same time wiping every tear from our eyes with the promise that 'Death will be no more; mourning and crying and pain will be no more' (Revelation 21.4).

As it tells us of God's first acts in making the world, the narrative in Genesis notes that he declared it to be 'good' and 'very good'. The point is sometimes made that he did not deem it to be 'perfect'. Perfection comes after the painstaking process of working with the raw material. Like a sculptor, God chips and chisels away, working with both the grain and the gremlins, with both the bloom and the blemishes. Sculpting justice through suffering and injustice is part of this sculptor's art, and this is the artistry that we see in Jesus' own life. He is the wounded healer, the servant who suffers, and the afflicted artist who is 'making all things new'. It seems that without having been totally immersed in, baptized by and fully acquainted with the suffering of this life, Jesus could not deal fully with the injustices and sins of the world and liberate God's creation.

Maybe that's why it was necessary for the Son of Man, the Child of the Earth, 'to be reckoned alongside transgressors' and 'to be delivered into the hands of sinful people and to be crucified and to rise again on the third day'. Maybe that's why 'the prophets foretold that it was necessary for Christ to suffer' and why it was 'necessary that these things should be fulfilled that were spoken in the Law of Moses, the Prophets and the Psalms' (Luke 22.37; 24.7, 25, 46, my translations).

Through Jesus, God made himself totally at one with his wounded world that had become estranged from him. God embraced injustice and all its unfair suffering at the cross of Christ and the whole of creation shuddered.

Postscript

In 1993 on 18 November, I was due to do 'Thought for the Day'. I had prepared a script about the NHS that had been signed off by the producer the night before. At six in the morning, I was called by the *Today* programme with the news of a terrible accident on the M40. A minibus with young people returning from a concert at the Royal Albert Hall had crashed and there were fatalities. In the car on the way to the studio, I composed the following.

'Thought for the Day', 18 November 1993

The mass that Father Kevin Kavanagh will celebrate at 9.00 this morning at Hagley High School will be the focus of the thoughts and prayers of very many people. As he stands there between earth and heaven, young people will no doubt be looking to him as a source of comfort. For, this morning, parents and young people of that Roman Catholic high school will come together to learn the names of children and friends who have been killed and learn, also, the awful truth of how fragile and how unpredictable life always is. Now words will fail these young people in their grief, as they do us in a sense. Stunned silence, wordless tears. These will be, for them, their food, day and night, for some time. For the parents of children who have died, there has already begun a period of intense busyness for which nothing in their life will have yet prepared them. As parents, we expect to be buried by our children; we don't expect to bury them ourselves.

In a book called *Lament for a Son* (William B. Eerdmans, 1996), Nicholas Wolterstorff writes about his own pain when his son was killed tragically in a mountaineering accident. In his own journey through grief, he wonders about God, and a friend reminds him of something from the Bible when it says that no one can look upon the face of God and live. He always thought, up until that moment, that this meant that no one could see the splendour of God and live. Until he realized that it might mean that no one could bear to see that face of God in sorrow, to see the tears in his eyes, and possibly live beyond this point.

Because, of course, to see the tears in the eyes of someone you love breaks the heart. You can steel yourself in the moment of grief, many people have done that, but the moment you see the tear-stained face of a close friend of someone you love, the tears begin to flow like a never-ending stream. The tears shed in Stourbridge today, the tears shed at Hagley High School, the tears that will be shed around the altar in the presence of Father Kavanagh, these tears we know have their source in the tear-filled eyes of God himself.

6

Race

When Enoch Powell made his infamous 'Rivers of blood' speech in Birmingham in 1968, I was in my first year of reading Theology at Exeter University. Powell quoted from Virgil's *Aeneid*: 'as I look ahead I am filled with foreboding; like the Roman I seem to see the River Tiber foaming with much blood.'

Powell had in his sights mass immigration, especially from the Commonwealth, and the proposed Race Relations Bill, which would make it illegal to refuse housing, employment or public services on grounds of colour, race or natural origins. The inflammatory image caused uproar. His next public speech was in the Great Hall at Exeter University. I was there. The hall was packed, the media were swarming and dotted around the walls were men standing in brown shirts. Fast-forward more than forty years, and I returned to the Great Hall to receive an honorary degree from the hands of the Chancellor of the university, Trinidadian British actor Baroness Floella Benjamin DBE. She insisted on hugging every single graduate. Within half a century of Enoch Powell's dire forecast, the River Exe flowed serenely through the university city as a black female chancellor embraced students of various colours and creeds.

In the 1980s, when I was a curate in Bristol, I listened to one of the leaders of our black-led churches talk of his coming to the country from the West Indies as one of the Windrush generation. As he was leaving, his mother told him to do three things when he arrived: 'First, find yourself a church so that you can thank God that you've arrived. Next, find yourself a friend. Then, go looking for a Post Office so you can write home and tell me you've arrived safely.' The black pastor then paused and added wistfully, 'Eventually I found the Post Office.' Even though they were filling vital jobs in our public services and contributing to the economy, these people met with huge hostility, which, in the end, for the sake of racial justice and harmony, had to be addressed by legislation and the Race Relations Bill to which Enoch Powell took such grave exception.

As my black pastor colleague found, the established Church was no less hostile and led to the formation of many black-led churches. I was invited to preach in one in the St Paul's area of Bristol. When the choir began singing 'We plough the fields and scatter' with the rhythms, cadences and harmonies of black gospel music, it split the atom of my soul. During the chorus of 'all good gifts around us are sent from Heaven above', I felt an exhilaration that I wished could go on for ever. In that moment and subsequently, I have marvelled at the grace of this worship. Taking lyrics and songs of the Church that had sanctioned the slavery of their ancestors and, until recently, had spurned their black presence in our white congregations, they had made these hymns their own and redeemed them.

In spite of the general and often subliminal hostility of the Church, there were certain leaders who spoke out about racial justice and argued for political change. But whenever faith leaders enter this territory, politicians often retort, especially if the criticism is a little too close to the bone, that religion should keep out of politics. Enoch Powell himself quoted Jesus as saying, 'My kingdom is not of this world' (John 18.36, KJV) as an argument that Church leaders should refrain from political comment. But a closer look at this saying of Jesus' shows that he means something very different. Standing in front of Pontius Pilate on a criminal and capital charge of sedition, Jesus was asked if he saw himself as a king, as 'king of the Jews'. Jesus didn't deny being a king. He said the source of his sovereignty did not lie with any human agency but came from above. In other words, 'My kingship does not come from this world but from God'. So much of what Jesus did and taught was about making a difference in this world; it proceeded from his own prayer for the coming of God's kingdom and for the earthing of heaven. It was about creating a just society. It was about enhancing the quality of life that would outlive death itself.

For me, the episode in Jesus' life that hit hardest at racial injustice was his cleansing of the Temple. At the heart of the Temple in Jerusalem was the holy of holies, where only the high priest could enter to offer sacrifices on the altar once a year on the Day of Atonement. People would come from all over to Jerusalem on religious festivals to worship and to bring their sacrifices.

These festivals, like the Passover and the Day of Atonement, were written deep into the history and the heart of the Jewish people, but they also had an appeal for others who were not born Jews. There was a part of the Temple set aside for them that came to be known as 'the Court of the Gentiles'. Over time, this area was taken over by traders, including stall-holders selling animals and birds for sacrifice, and money-changers dealing in Temple and foreign currency for those travelling from afar. There was nothing wrong with any of this business, but there was a problem with where they were doing it. By taking over the Court of the Gentiles, they were denying the foreign pilgrims their dedicated space in which to worship God, the reason for which they had travelled so far. Defying again any image of meekness and mildness, Jesus turned the stalls over, drove out the culprits and refused to let anyone carry anything through the Temple Court. He restored to the Gentiles their sacred space. It caused a sensation. It made the religious leaders even more determined to kill him, but he turned to the Bible to explain his actions: 'My house shall be called a house of prayer for all the nations . . . But you have made it a den of robbers' (Mark 11.17).

Jesus was quoting from two prophets of old, Isaiah and Jeremiah. By robbing the Gentiles of their sacred space to worship God, the Temple authorities were undermining the principle and promise that the Temple should be a house of prayer for everybody. Not just for the Jews but for the Gentiles as well. Their action was discriminatory and sacrilegious. It required Jesus to call it out. It was unjust. It was, in effect, racist.

What I find remarkable, and indeed something that may have served to reinforce racism, is that for 2,000 years Christians have concentrated on the 'den of robbers' and largely ignored the racial dimension of Jesus' explanation. Jesus was drawing on an inclusive vision from the prophet Isaiah:

> And the foreigners who join themselves to the LORD,
> to minister to him, to love the name of the LORD,
> and to be his servants,
> all who keep the sabbath, and do not profane it,
> and hold fast my covenant –
> these I will bring to my holy mountain,
> and make them joyful in my house of prayer;
> their burnt offerings and their sacrifices
> will be accepted on my altar;
> for my house shall be called a house of prayer
> for all peoples.
> (Isaiah 56.6–7)

The vision could not be clearer! God has no favourites. The outsider becomes an insider; the foreigner becomes a friend. The Temple is home to all who pray to God, whatever their ethnic origin. He is a God without prejudice and without boundaries, a God without frontiers. And if that were not clear enough from the prophet Isaiah, Jesus quoted also from the prophet Jeremiah: 'Has this house, which is called by my name, become a den of robbers? You know, I too am watching' (Jeremiah 7.11).

This warning comes after Jeremiah has castigated the people for their injustices and encouraged them to mend their ways: 'If you truly act justly one with another, if you do not oppress the alien, the orphan and the widow . . . then I will dwell with you in this place' (Jeremiah 7.5–8). Turning the Temple into a den of robbers, oppressing and robbing the alien Gentiles of their space to worship the God of Abraham was an injustice that met with Jesus' wrath. He was what Jeremiah described elsewhere as being 'full of the wrath of the Lord' (Jeremiah 6.11).

Admittedly, this was a difficult message for both Jews and the Jewish Christians to accept, as Peter explained: 'You yourselves know that it is unlawful for a Jew to associate with or to visit a Gentile; but God has shown me that I should not call anyone profane or unclean.' He went further: 'I truly understand that God shows no partiality, but in every nation anyone who fears him and does what is right is acceptable to him . . . Jesus Christ . . . is Lord of all' (Acts 10.28, 34–37).

Although Peter didn't always see eye to eye with Paul, they were nevertheless agreed on this point: 'In Christ Jesus you are all children of God through faith. As many of you as were baptized into Christ have clothed yourselves with Christ. There is no longer Jew or Greek, there is no longer slave or free, there is no longer male or female; for all of you are one in Christ Jesus' (Galatians 3.26–28).

In the first century this was the most radical breaking down of racial, class and gender barriers, and it was fundamental to the possibility of creating a just society one day in which everybody has a responsibility to respect the rights of the other. Even though these thoughts were written 2,000 years ago, racism remains part of the shadow side of human nature. Its animus threatens and thwarts the realization of a just and harmonious society.

In Liverpool there has been a black presence and community for well over 200 years. It is a legacy of the slave trade triangle, in which slaves were shipped from West Africa to the east coast of America via Liverpool, in exchange for cotton and sugar. But during my fifteen years in Liverpool, owning its past and integrating its black and minority ethnic communities was at best a work in progress for the city. Sometimes an ugly incident would erupt and expose the city's shadow side.

Anthony Walker was a talented eighteen-year-old Scouser. Black. He had a great future ahead of him and an ambition to be a lawyer. He was set upon in a racist attack by thugs, who murdered him in a park with an axe to his head. He was a Christian. His mother, Gee, told me about the racism they encountered both before and after Anthony's murder. His killers were convicted and went to prison unrepentant. To Gee's own surprise and consternation, she heard herself speaking about forgiving them because she wanted to follow the example of Jesus and because she did not want to be consumed by hatred. Anthony's murder showed that there is a racism that continues to lurk in our human subconscious. It is not limited to white on black. It manifests itself in different colours and is a constant threat to our wish to live in a just and harmonious world. It is insidious because it can be both conscious and subconscious. It can be both personal and institutional.

All the above was written just before the killing of George Floyd in America. We are not the only nation to be afflicted by the disease of racism. George Floyd's murder in police custody in Minneapolis in 2020 has become a tipping point in our awareness of racial discrimination worldwide and, in particular, of the historic subjugation of black people by white. Even though African tribal chiefs themselves colluded with and profited from the slave trade across the Atlantic, and even though this was preceded by the Arab trading of slaves across the Sahara, nothing mitigates the barbarous cruelty of enslavement and trafficking. John Newton, the author of the poem that came to be known as the hymn 'Amazing Grace', was the only slave ship captain to give evidence to Parliament on the evils of the slave trade. His testimony was harrowing and included accounts of insurgent slaves being hanged, drawn and quartered. When he was shipwrecked off the coast of Ireland, he turned to Christ. He became a tide surveyor in Liverpool and then a priest in the Church of England. He was a great influence in the life of William Wilberforce, whom he encouraged to hold fast to the campaign to abolish the slave trade in the face of fierce opposition in Parliament and in the country. It has taken over 200 years for the media to grasp that black lives matter as much as those of every other colour. We are now beginning to look at our history through the eyes not just of those who wrote it and were the subjects of it but also of those who were the objects of evil deeds that were done.

The current movement is raising fundamental questions about our historic monuments and memorials, about our statues and our statutes, about our culture and our constitution. Arguments rage about whether or not we should take down memorials of those historic figures who played such a prominent role in our imperial past. Civic and military leaders marched through the chapters of our history to the drumbeat of a very different set of values. A major grievance of those who are black, Asian or of a non-white ethnicity is that they have been written out of the history books. It seems to me that to take down the memorials of those who have oppressed others quite literally pushes them off their pedestals, but in the process further airbrushes from our history their role in our past. The fact that racist individuals accumulated so much wealth on the backs of black people, and were honoured, is part of our uncomfortable history. We should be confronted by such an inconvenient truth and not be protected from its offensiveness. But the other aspect of the disturbing presence of these monuments is that a human being has the capacity for both cruelty and kindness. The world does not divide neatly into saints and sinners, the just and the unjust. Human nature is much more multifaceted than that. The kindest can be cruel and the cruel can be kind. It gives us a mirror to look into and to see the truth about ourselves. And if we wish to counterpoint the honour that was given by previous generations, then let us build new monuments to honour those who have striven for justice, laboured for equality and died for freedom. Let us build them side by side and tell the next chapter of our common story.

Addressing and judging our past should make us conscious of the present by asking how future generations will judge our current values. Imagine a world where a deadly virus has affected our fertility; how will moral attitudes change towards the unborn child? Imagine a world that has not sufficiently heeded the warnings about carbon emissions that have led to devastating sea level rise; how will moral attitudes regard this era of careless consumption? In a world in which it is harder to breathe because of increasingly toxic pollution, how will moral attitudes change concerning the untamed individualism evident in our transport and housing? These should give us reason to pause and make a sober judgement of our own behaviour. As to our current attitudes to race and inequality, what we need, according to Trevor Phillips, former Chair of the Equality and Human Rights Commission, is proper data to analyse and assess the trends and bias in our institutions. He makes the point that engineers do not go about building a bridge by reading stories about crossing bridges; they need facts and figures, dimensions and designs. We need the data that comes from scientific analysis in order to address the injustices inherent in society that impede the full participation of all ethnic groups in our national life. It is a sobering thought that the disdain with which we rightly look on the racial attitudes of former generations might pale when future social historians examine our moral complacency in failing to address in our lifetime the ethical issues and injustices that will dominate the next century.

Postscript

'Thought for the Day', 27 July 2020

On Thursday this week, it'll be the fifteenth anniversary of the murder of Anthony Walker, and tonight, on BBC 1, Jimmy McGovern's play, *Anthony*, will tell the story of the life he never got to live.

I led Anthony's funeral in Liverpool's Anglican cathedral, and last year on Good Friday I interviewed his mother, Gee Walker, here on Radio 4. When I asked her to describe him, she said, 'He was just every mother's dream child. Thank God he gave me everything I ask for. Tall, dark, handsome. Sensitive. Loved me, loved God, loved people.'

Gee wanted him to be a preacher; Anthony wanted to be a lawyer. He used to taunt his teachers with a cheeky grin: 'Go on, Miss. Smile. Have a nice day!' He was fit and strong. No one would mess with him. Except one night: on 29 July 2005, Michael Barton and Paul Taylor hurled racist abuse at him and his friends at a bus stop in Huyton, and Taylor sank an ice axe into Anthony's head.

When Gee got to the hospital and insisted on seeing him, she told me all she had to do was to follow his blood: 'His blood led me to him.' By this time, Gee had got hundreds of people all over the world praying for him, but he never regained consciousness and died.

When I asked her, 'What did that do to your faith?' I didn't expect what followed. 'That increased my faith because I realized that now all I've got is God.'

I wish I could replay the whole sixty minutes we recorded. Or, better still, see the full three-score years and ten that Anthony should have lived. For he had the faith and the values of his mother.

As I've looked back over the last twenty-seven years, and the deaths of Stephen Lawrence, Damilola Taylor and Anthony Walker, I've wondered why it's taken the killing of an unknown man in Minneapolis to make us in this country 'take the knee'. Why did not the murder of three of our own black teenagers drive us to our knees?

As I've watched Anthony's mother – her willingness to forgive, her refusal to be consumed by hatred – I've wondered if we've presumed too much on the decency of the Lawrences, the Taylors and the Walkers. On this programme, Gee Walker said she hoped the play tonight would 'honour' Anthony. Unlike a statue, it'll make him come alive, breathing life back into his wounded body.

It'll be a vindication – and a resurrection.

7

Islam

For the first part of my life, the dominant tension in the world was between capitalism and communism. The threat of nuclear war loomed over us like an atomic cloud. The tumbling down of the Berlin Wall marked the beginning of the liberation of the East from totalitarianism and the West from the fear of nuclear catastrophe. Yet, the communist–capitalist conflict was but a blip on the geopolitical map of the world of the last millennium. For about a century it displaced the much more dominant and historic tension between Islam and Christianity, which has now reasserted itself in different forms to shape not only Europe but also the whole world. Each day it undermines harmony internationally, nationally and locally.

In each religious tradition there is a spectrum of belief between the two polarities of enlightened faith and defiant bigotry. This is not limited to Christianity and Islam and can be found in the other great beliefs, such as Hinduism and Buddhism. Christian and Islamic cultures rely heavily on the interpretation of the sacred texts of the Bible and the Qur'an. The questions facing faith leaders in the twenty-first century is whether or not they feel a responsibility to interpret these texts with integrity. Will they seek to find common ground between the religions? Will they apply the principles of justice and mercy, distilled from their sacred writings, to build relationships of mutual respect and to work together towards a more harmonious world? The future stability of the world depends on it.

There is a long way to go because, within these two cultures of Islam and Christianity, there are some who are locked into a binary mentality in which both sides are, paradoxically, dominated by a unified vision of the future of the Earth entailing its destruction. Reading from both the Bible and the Qur'an, certain fundamentalists of both faiths subscribe to what has been called 'a theology of obliteration'. Relying on passages from their Scriptures, they believe that the world will come to an end and God will replace it with a paradise for faithful believers. Although this summary runs the danger of oversimplification, their creed means that you can milk the Earth for all its worth before the world comes to an end, and if your actions, politically and militarily, serve to bring about a conflagration, then their attitude is to say, 'Bring it on', because this is what the sacred texts prophesy. It's as if the two cultures of the Christianized West and the Muslim world are engaged in a cold war of their own, with theological missiles trained on each other, a situation that will end in mutually assured destruction to be followed by a paradise for the victors. That may sound a caricature, but there are many religious people in America and as many religious adherents in the Arab world and elsewhere whose political ideology is informed by such readings of the Bible and the Qur'an.

The tragedy is that it spawns a dangerous demonization and division along religious, and even racial, lines and leads to oppression of one side by the other. So, in the West, Muslims can find themselves despised and treated with suspicion and disdain; and in predominantly Muslim countries, Christians can find themselves brutally persecuted and denied the freedom to practise their faith.

For most of my time as Bishop of Liverpool, the leader of the Muslim community was Dr Muhammad Akbar Ali. We became friends and worked together closely when, in September

2004, Ken Bigley, who originally hailed from Liverpool, was kidnapped by terrorists in Iraq. We pleaded together in Arabic and English to save his life. Together, in Walton Parish Church, we held a vigil. In the vestry, we found ourselves praying together. It was the first time that I had knowingly prayed with a Muslim. I was very conscious of this and yet, in the circumstances, and given the bond between us, cemented by our common faith in God, theological questions were swept aside by the unfolding tragedy. Ken Bigley was then cruelly and tragically murdered in the name of Islam, which deeply distressed Akbar and me. That night, the police prioritized the protection of mosques on Merseyside in case there were reprisals. In the event, there were only a few minor incidents. Akbar and I hoped, but will never know, that our public as well as our private friendship mitigated some of the hostile reaction to such barbaric violence.

The oldest mosque in the UK is in Woking, but the oldest Islamic prayer room is to be found in Liverpool. William Henry Quilliam, a local lawyer, converted to Islam on his travels to North Africa in 1887 and turned 8 Brougham Terrace into a prayer room and then into a mosque. More than 100 years later, the Muslim community sought to restore it and develop it as an education and heritage centre of British Islam.

They asked me, as the Bishop of Liverpool, to be one of the patrons of their enterprise. I was honoured by this vote of friendship, but exercised by the theological implications. Christianity and Islam unite in a belief in the mercy of God, but diverge on three key points of faith: the Trinity of God, the divinity of Jesus and the historicity of his crucifixion. Yet, I eventually decided that I could accept their invitation without compromising my own faith or the convictions of my Muslim hosts, on the basis of the second great commandment, which is to love your neighbour as yourself. I braced myself for opposition, especially when I told the story on 'Thought for the Day' in the *Today* programme on Radio 4, but there was only one objection, which Akbar and I took as a hopeful sign. We still had to wrestle with the theological questions but, as with all doctrinal debates, this was better done as friends rather than as enemies.

I discovered that the term 'Islam' did not feature in the earliest period of the faith, but emerged as a religious and socio-political ideology only later. Followers of Jesus Christ were embraced by early Muslims as fellow People of the Book.

I came to understand more about the origin of key Islamic doctrines: how the emphasis on the Oneness of God had been a reaction to the polytheism that was developing around Christianity in the Middle East in the seventh century; how the denial of the crucifixion of Jesus emerged in a culture that could not believe a truly merciful God would allow his favoured servant to suffer. This last question is new every morning to all people of faith. How can we believe in a loving God when so many bad things happen to good people? The Muslim disbelief that God could allow Jesus to suffer so cruelly on the cross is counter-pointed by the hope, shared by both Muslims and Christians, that the same God will one day bring an end to all suffering, to crying and dying and grieving.

When Theresa May was Prime Minister, my wife and I were invited by her and Mr May to an informal dinner at Chequers one Saturday evening. After dinner she took us to the long gallery for coffee. There, set on a table on its own, was a copy of the Qur'an in English. Mrs May told me that it was the first book she had serendipitously pulled off the shelf when she first went into the library. Published in 1734, it was translated by George Sale, a British orientalist and solicitor, and dedicated to a member of the Privy Council to show that Islam was not the rogue religion some had made it out to be.

I found it fascinating for several reasons. Sale's work showed that Islam is not a recent interloper into our culture, and, in spite of tensions 200 years ago, there were advocates in high places prepared to challenge the prevailing religious prejudice and seek a fair settlement for a different religion.

The Ecumenical Patriarch of Constantinople, Bartholomew I, regularly hosted an annual symposium in different parts of the world to highlight the global ecological challenges that face us. I was asked to join a gathering of scientists and faith leaders in Manaus, Brazil, to study the impact of deforestation on the Amazon – both forest and river. We spent a week sailing up the river deep into the forest, listening to presentations from different scientific and religious perspectives. Conscious of the environmental impact of our own travelling as we all flew there from Lisbon, I, nevertheless, found the encounter with native tribes and local communities incomparable to any film, book or article in understanding the ecological crisis facing the world. The destruction of the trees, the lungs of the Earth, takes your breath away both physically and metaphorically. At the start of the journey, there was a presentation that took my breath away from a spiritual point of view. It was by Dr Nariman Gasimoglu, a Muslim scholar from the University of Baku in Azerbaijan. He expounded the Muslim ethic of caring for God's creation, based on the Qur'an.

His words put a song in my heart. We spent time talking on our own. I was particularly intrigued by his reference to what the Qur'an has to say about the role of Jesus on the Day of Judgement, also called 'The Hour' (43.61). It seemed to me to have a resonance with the saying of Jesus in Matthew's Gospel when 'at the renewal of all things the Child of the Earth will be seated on the throne of his glory' (19.28, my translation).

Some time after we had all returned home, a package arrived from Azerbaijan. It contained two issues of the *Journal of Azerbaijani Studies* with an article by Nariman on the 'Commonalities in Bible and Koran from ecotheology perspectives', in which he compares our two presentations in Manaus and shows how much we had in common as we both advocated ways of caring for the Earth, while drawing on our own sacred texts. Nariman also notes that, in spite of work by many Muslim scholars, 'the current religious mindset of the Muslim majority is not sensitive to ecological issues' (No. 3, p. 18). It is a situation paralleled by the Christian community. Nariman then offered a critique of both my lecture and my book *Jesus and the Earth*, in which I expounded the significance of the Lord's Prayer as a plea for the earthing of heaven.

Nariman, as a translator of the Azeri Qur'an, offers this commentary on my thesis:

[T]hese comments are in full compliance with corresponding Koranic verses, which require that both worldly and hereafter life balance out in the religious thought and practice as believers are called to pray before God uttering; 'Our Lord! Give us good in this world and good in the hereafter . . .
(No. 3, p. 21)

In his paper he goes on to argue that the greater our faith, the deeper will be our appreciation of our environment: 'The reason why everything we contemplate in the environment – forests, meadows, mountain heights covered with snow – looks so beautiful is conditioned by God's seal and paint [which] they all bear in their capacity as His creatures.' He later quotes the Qur'an: 'who is better than God at painting? And Him do we serve' (2.138), and comments, 'The suggestion here is that we take into consideration the beauty, harmony and equilibrium He has set for the life of both human beings and the earth as a whole' (No. 3, p. 35).

These passages from the Qur'an and Nariman's commentary signified three things for me. First, in both the Bible and the Qur'an there are passages which explicitly express the view that an ecological balance is essential to a harmonious and just world. Second, there is indisputably common ground in the fundamental tenets regarding God's creation between Islam and Christianity – and Judaism. Third, it is only by a determined seeking of mutual understanding that we can overcome the prejudices and discrimination of religion and race, which are so often fed by our need for tribal security. The prize of so doing is a more stable world; the penalty of failure risks mutually assured destruction and obliteration. Over the last ten years, my long-distance friendship with Nariman has deepened. We sign off to each other with 'Your friend in faith', ever more conscious of what binds us together across religion and race. I have learnt so much from him, not least a deepening of my understanding of God's relationship with the animal world. It's there in the Bible in Psalm 104 and it's equally there in the Qur'an. Commenting on sura 25, verses 45-49, 'We send down pure water from the sky – that with it We may give life to a dead land, and slake in rich portion the thirst of what We have created as cattle and men', Nariman writes, 'In God's eyes humans and animals have equal rights when it comes to sharing water He sends down from the sky' (No. 4, p. 29).

Nariman later adds, 'The Koran calls on human beings not to overlook the fact that just as God communicated with human messengers, so He did with bees' (No. 4, p. 35), again quoting the Qur'an: 'And you Lord revealed to the bee saying: Make hives in the mountains and in the trees . . . then eat of all the fruits and walk in the ways of your Lord submissively. There comes forth from within it a beverage of many colours, in which there is healing for men' (16.68–69).

These verses put me in mind of a poem by George Herbert, 'Providence', which celebrates the role of the bee in the way God sustains his creation:

Bees work for man; and yet they never bruise
Their master's flower, but leave it, having done,
As fair as ever, and as fit to use;
So both the flower doth stay and honey run.

Much of the conversation between us has centred on Jesus. Nariman warmed to my exposition of Jesus as the Son of Man or Child of the Earth, and of his role in ushering in God's kingdom. Although Jesus blessed his followers when they acknowledged him as Lord, the title that he himself used more than any other was Child of the Earth. I have found in conversation with Muslims that following Jesus' own example and referring to him in this way creates a more open space for dialogue.

Nariman's own devotion to Jesus has moved me as much as his deep ecological understanding. Both are exemplified in this poem, translated by Nariman from Turkic, which he has given me permission to publish:

See this is me on water reflecting on the universe
With my soul that has left my body in another time.
A heavenly breeze gives this a gleaming smile
That waves to thaw all the frozen lights.
Behold, how sun landing on this illuminates my soul
And I find it setting in my reflection to float as a halo.
This halo is reflected on water to shape my reflection into
    a pair.

Behold, who has become my bosom friend as a word for
   friends to utter.
Isn't this Jesus Christ who walks on water tramping across
   my reflection?
And my eyes flutter open into an enchanting beauty.
Tie me up, o my Lord, to His feet and raise me up
So my reflection rising from water will rain on earth in
   myriad drops.
The rain is falling to tie the heavens down to earth,
O my Lord, hit these falling strings with Gasimoglu in your
   hand.

In the New Testament, we see Jesus destined to become a universal figure, a focus of faith for people of every race. At the end of Matthew's Gospel, after his resurrection, Jesus directs his followers to take his teachings to other nations. His message was not to be confined to one people. It was a global gospel of love from whose fountain cascaded both justice and mercy.

This mission was consistent with the insights revealed after his birth in the opening chapters of Luke's Gospel, where Simeon, a 'just and devout' man (Luke 2.25, KJV), took the baby Jesus in his arms and blessed him for being not just 'the glory of your people Israel' but also 'a light for revelation to the nations' (Luke 2.32, my translation), a person of faith to be trusted by both Jew and Gentile. Simeon surprised Mary and Joseph with this prophecy and began to prepare them for how costly it would be for them all: 'and a sword will pierce your own soul too' (Luke 2.35). All this happened in the Temple in Jerusalem, where, some thirty years later, Jesus would empty the Court of the Gentiles set apart for the other God-fearing nationals with the rousing challenge, 'My house shall be called a house of prayer for all the nations'. He restored to them their sacred space, of which they had been robbed by those who had turned it into a 'den of robbers' (Mark 11.17).

It brings to mind another episode from the Gospels in which Jesus commends the faith of a Roman centurion who asks him to heal one of his servants by just saying the word. Although he was a foreigner, Jesus said that he had not found such a faith in all Israel and went on to add, 'many will come from east and west, and will eat with Abraham and Isaac and Jacob in the kingdom of heaven' (Matthew 8.11). It reinforced the vision of Isaiah 56.6–7, where the Lord welcomes all nations with Israel on his Holy Mount, which was later superimposed by the vision of St Peter, who heard God say, 'I should not call anyone profane or unclean . . . I truly understand that God shows no partiality, but in every nation anyone who fears and does what is right is acceptable to him' (Acts 10.28, 34–35). Reading this manuscript before publication, Nariman remarked on the similarity with the Qur'anic verse: 'O mankind, indeed, We have created you male and female, and have made you into nations and tribes that you may know one another. Indeed, the noblest of you in the sight of God is the most righteous of you. Surely, God is All-knowing and All-aware' (49.13).

I have been to Jerusalem only once. I stood on the Mount of Olives and looked out over the city. I removed my shoes and walked in the hallowed space under the Dome of the Rock, where I prayed silently for Nariman. I donned a white kippah, or yarmulke, to make my pilgrimage and prayers at the Wailing Wall on the site of the second Temple. I held the key to the Church of the Holy Sepulchre and entered the tomb revered as the burial place of Jesus.

Each of those three sites, although representative of three different religions, intensifies the sense of holiness of the others. They can be interpreted as symbols of strife historically, in the present and into the future, but each is also a symbol of the earthing of heaven. Simon Sebag Montefiore, in the epilogue in his book *Jerusalem: The biography* (Weidenfeld & Nicholson, 2011), captures the significance of these places:

> It is now one hour before dawn on a day in Jerusalem. The Dome of the Rock is open: Muslims are praying. The Wall is always open: the Jews are praying. The Church of the Holy Sepulchre is open: the Christians are praying in several languages. The sun is rising over Jerusalem, its rays making the light Herodian stones of the Wall almost snowy – just as Josephus described it two thousand years ago – and then catching the glorious gold of the Dome of the Rock that glints back at the sun. The divine esplanade where Heaven and Earth meet, where God meets man, is still in a realm beyond human cartography.

Sadly, it is true that some purists of each of the three Abrahamic religions are not comfortable with the presence of the others on the Holy Mount. It is their fervent hope, indeed the prayer of some, that the others will one day vanish or be vanquished. But ever since I set eyes on the Holy Mount, I have been in conversation with this passage that Jesus quoted from Isaiah about 'the foreigners who join themselves to the LORD, to minister to him, to love the name of the LORD, and to be his servants . . . these I will bring to my holy mountain, and make them joyful in my house of prayer . . . for my house shall be called a house of prayer for all peoples' (Isaiah 56.6–7).

Although it is a profoundly uneasy settlement in every sense of that phrase, the coexistence of the three holy sites and their appeal to believers of every nation make this Holy Mount a unique and 'divine esplanade where Heaven and Earth meet' for countless millions. It is an ironic fulfilment of Isaiah's prophecy that all – Jew and Christian and Muslim – do now find a place on God's Holy Mount, albeit amid huge tensions. But the reason that I have gone down this path in a book about justice is that I believe substantial common ground can be found between the Judeo-Christian and Islamic traditions in our understanding of both justice and mercy. In order to guard our world from the destructive polarization of religions through the corruption of faith by sectarian groups and terrorists, we would do well to consider all that the Abrahamic faiths share, and how Islam, Judaism and Christianity embrace the moral imperative to act justly and the divine grace to be merciful.

Again, I am indebted to my friend Nariman, who notes that in the text of the Qur'an, 'the beautiful names of God' include 'al-Adl' (the Just) and 'Rahman' (the Most Merciful). They are indeed beautiful.

In sura 4, verse 135, there is a call to all believers to 'stand out firmly for justice as witnesses to Allah even as against yourselves or your parents or your kin and whether it be (against) rich or poor'. There are warnings against distorting and declining to do justice, which echo the outspokenness of the Jewish prophets. In the same sura, there are resonances with Jesus' own teaching, that when 'ye judge between man and man that ye judge with justice' (4.58). We also read about the relationship between faith and justice in ways that, again, are familiar to both Jews and Christians: 'O ye who believe! Stand out firmly for Allah as witnesses to fair dealing . . . Be just: that is next to Piety; and fear Allah for Allah is well acquainted with all that you do' (5.8), and: 'If thou judge, judge in equity between them; for Allah loveth those who judge with equity' (5.42).

Alongside 'Rahman', among 'the beautiful names of God', is 'Rahim', meaning the 'Bestower of Mercy'. All the suras of the Qur'an except one begin by invoking God as 'The Most Merciful, the Bestower of Mercy'. As in the New Testament, there is an emphasis in the Qur'an on believers receiving the mercy of God and in turn spreading kindness and mercy in the name of Rahman, the 'Most Merciful'.

None of this is to overlook the differences between Judaism, Christianity and Islam, nor am I proposing a syncretism that blurs the distinctiveness of each faith. But it does unearth foundations in all three faiths that expose common ground on which we can strive to build an ethic of justice and mercy that satisfies the universal moral instinct to be found in every human conscience to be both fair and forgiving.

Postscript

'Thought for the Day', 29 October 2001

The murder of Christians in Pakistan while they were worshipping God fills me with grief, and leaves you wondering what the next atrocity will be.

Shortly after September 11 2001, the leaders of the Pakistani Muslims in Liverpool came to see me. They were concerned for Pakistan, and for the impact of its involvement in the war on the Pakistani community here in the UK.

The fact is that, in this cosmopolitan world, shrunken by the media into a suburb, distance has been eliminated. There is no such thing as 'abroad' or 'overseas' any more. Every event has an impact locally. The destruction of the World Trade Centre, the bombings of Afghanistan, the tension between Islam and Christianity are felt by all of us everywhere like tremors of an earthquake. Globalization has already happened. It's a fact.

Last year, I was in Nigeria, which has just witnessed another bout of violence – this time involving the military. Everywhere I went, the children shouted out 'Wanibo' – 'white man'. The innocent laughter on the children's faces made it all the more difficult to believe that violence also stalked those streets down which they ran so joyfully.

One of the conflicts in Nigeria sadly is between Islam and Christianity. Christians and Muslims have killed each other, with mosques and churches being burned to the ground. One of the issues is the desire of the Muslim community to incorporate Sharia law into the State's legislation. This is being resisted by Christians and those who value Nigeria's recent return to democratic government.

But what impressed me was the leadership being given by the Anglican Bishop of Kaduna. With the courage of that other African Anglican, Desmond Tutu, he was calling on Christians, whose churches had been burnt down, to turn first and rebuild the mosques that had been razed to the ground. The Christian Bishop Josiah raising money to build again Muslim centres of worship, even though he believes there are fundamental differences between the two faiths.

It's that sort of leadership the world needs.

I heard it again when last week I met a leading Pakistani Christian. He told me of how, just now, it was the Muslim leaders in his part of Pakistan who were promising protection to the Christian communities who had served them with schools and hospitals for generations.

Tomorrow, the Prime Minister will be addressing the Welsh Assembly and, according to the press briefing, will assure us that our 'moral fibre' will defeat the terrorists. Muslims and Christians both agree with the Prime Minister that those who take innocent life ought to be arrested and punished. The moral fibres that need now to be woven together are seen in those who sit with one arm tearfully around the victim and with the other stretched out to the violators – whoever they are – with the words of Jesus straining and stretching every muscle, 'Love your enemy and pray for those who persecute you'.

8

Prison

In Altcourse Prison just outside Liverpool, I sat in the audience watching a play. It had been improvised by twelve offenders. It was called *The Choice* and was about the decision that all prisoners have to make about how they will use their time inside. The plot centred on whether or not to do drugs. It didn't feel like a play. It felt as if someone had just taken off the prison wall to let us see what was going on in real time.

At the end of the play, the cast came forward to take a bow, then, one by one, each stepped further forwards and stepped out of character to confess to the audience what it was that each of them had done to end up in prison. The audience had already been gripped. They were now clamped to their seats. The lead (let's call him Wayne) told his story. He made no excuses. He kept saying that he shouldn't have done what he did. He kept repeating that, once he was out, he was never coming back. His story went something like this.

I never knew my dad. My mum used to bring back different 'uncles'. Some would beat her up. I used to get so angry. I couldn't do anything about it. I got so mad. When I was eighteen, I went to stay with my sister. One night, her boyfriend started hitting her and punching her in the head. Something inside me just snapped. I laid into him. I nearly killed him. I got sent down for Grievous Bodily Harm.

That fateful night, all his pent up fury at not being able to defend his mum erupted and all but turned him into a murderer. He kept saying that he knew he had done wrong, that he deserved to be in prison, but everyone in the audience knew that there, but for the grace of God, . . .

The cast then came down into the audience and sat in small groups to talk about the play. That's when the real action started. The audience was made up of some of the most challenging kids in Merseyside who could already see themselves in the play and in the men sitting alongside them. Their questions came thick and fast.

I do not want to excuse the crimes any more than Wayne did, but I do want to acknowledge that the ground which leads some to be in prison and others to be free is far from level or fair. The reason we have juries and judges and not just robots convicting and sentencing is to allow for humanity to be exercised in the administration of justice.

This was one of many prisons that I visited during my tenure as Bishop to Her Majesty's Prisons. Very early on, one of the chaplains set out an important question very clearly for me: are prisons simply to be warehouses for storing the incorrigible or will they become greenhouses to restore the redeemable? That's it in a nutshell. Whichever prison I went into, this question became the yardstick by which to measure it. Whichever approach was adopted was the result of a binary choice. It also reveals what we believe about human nature. Can the exercise of justice lead to redemption?

On the Isle of Sheppey, I spent several hours in one prison alone with twelve men convicted of murder. They had enlisted in an educational programme to understand not just the impact of crime generally but also the impact of their own crime on their victims. One murderer told me the effect the course was having on him: 'I had no idea that killing that person would do so much harm to so many.' On one level, it seemed such a crass and naive thing to say; but on another, as I looked into his face, he sounded utterly sincere and truthful. He had had no idea of the brutal damage and devastation he had caused.

There's a Chinese fable about an elderly barren couple who were granted two wishes by a genie. Immediately, they asked for a child. 'Granted', said the genie. Then they asked that the child should never feel any pain. The genie cautioned them: 'Oh no. Not that. Think again. I'll return after a month to hear what you have decided.' When he came back, the couple were unmoved and insisted on their two wishes. Both were granted. The story ends with the elderly parents not living long enough to see their longed-for child grow up to become the greatest tyrant the land had ever seen. The fact that he could not feel the pain of others turned him into a heartless and cruel ogre.

It's true that there are human beings who lack the facility to imagine the impacts that their actions have on others. This is why the development of the imagination is so vital to a child and young person's education. Having the ability to imagine and to put yourself in the shoes of someone else is key to nurturing a compassionate society. A curriculum devoid of drama, music, art and poetry fails to develop the imagination of the young, and makes them less sensitive to the needs of others. The arts are the vitamins for making a civilized world.

The word 'imagination' is to be found in the old English translation of the Bible, what we know as the 'Authorized Version'. Unfortunately, it appears only ever in a negative sense, such as, 'God saw that the wickedness of man was great in the earth, and that every imagination of the thoughts of his heart was only evil continually' (Genesis 6.5, KJV). According to the theologian John McIntyre, however, that ability to imagine and to put yourself in the shoes of others is a virtue that belongs to God himself. He argues that the divine imagination was a necessary prelude to the incarnation. It was only because God could project and imagine what it must be like to be oppressed by evil and tempted by sin that he could enter the world and address the issues of injustice which are their consequence. One consequence of being made in the image of God is that we have the potential to imagine.

Such an exercising of the imagination is evident in the thousands of groups, locally and nationally, that work constantly and independently in prisons rehabilitating offenders. Many of them are motivated by faith. Mick and Lyn Connolly's son Paul was murdered on the streets of Liverpool. He was innocent. The murder was senseless. They have since spent their lives going into prisons and meeting offenders to tell their story: the shock, the trauma, the bereavement, the desolation, the journey of grief without destination, the decision to forgive. They founded Impact, a charity that develops restorative justice programmes in prisons.

I've sat in a prison watching them tell their heartbreaking story to murderers and hardened criminals who have listened reluctantly, with their heads down, arms folded, legs crossed. I've watched those same heads lift and arms unfold as Lynn enters their world. I've seen the letters that they have sent her, tear-stained and crumpled, because her testimony as a bereft mother has touched them more deeply than the sentence itself. I've read letters written by prisoners in which, for the first time, they've offered the word 'sorry'. It's what is called restorative justice. Retributive justice is both an end in itself and a means to an end. It is punishment to fit the crime. It is deserved. It is the just outcome of wrongdoing. If it were not deserved, society would have no right to deny the person his or her liberty. But it can also prove to be a path to redemption.

One of the many things that the COVID crisis has shone a light on is how enforced and prolonged isolation suffocates the human spirit. It has given us an unexpected connection with those in prison. Up until the pandemic, the argument that punishment by imprisonment was the deprivation of liberty was one that to most people felt theoretical. It failed to convince many. Since the experience of lockdown, that argument is no longer theoretical. Millions have felt for themselves the painful impact, not least on our mental well-being, of being more or less imprisoned in our own homes. It has given us some insight into how incarceration and the consequent deprivation of liberty are bitter experiences and painfully punitive.

If incarceration itself is the just punishment that fits the crime, then the ground is clearer to ask what else can be achieved while serious offenders are locked up? In the case of dangerous offenders, prison also offers necessary protection to the public, but there's another purpose that can serve the interests of both the offended and the offender, as well as society as a whole: rehabilitation.

In the film *The Shawshank Redemption*, Red appears before the parole board for the third time to see if he's to be 'rehabilitated'.

Red: Well, now let me see. You know, I don't have any idea what that means.

Parole man: Well, it means that you're ready to rejoin society.

Red: I know what you think it means, sonny. To me, it's just a made up word. A politician's word, so that young fellas like yourself can wear a suit and a tie and have a job. What do you really want to know? Am I sorry for what I did?

Parole man: Well, are you?

Red: There's not a day goes by I don't feel regret. Not because I'm in here, or because you think I should. I look back on the way I was then, a young stupid

kid who committed that terrible crime. I want to
talk to him. I want to try to talk some sense into
him, tell him the way things are, but I can't. That
kid's long gone and this old man is all that's left.
I got to live with that. Rehabilitated? It's just a
bullshit word. So you go and stamp your forms,
sonny, and stop wasting my time. Because to tell
you the truth, I don't give a shit.

There's more talk about rehabilitation today, but sadly very
little of what goes on inside prisons actually rehabilitates prisoners.

Prisons fail both the offended and the offenders, and society
is badly served as ex-offenders on release become reoffenders.
The exceptions are the restorative justice programmes that lead
to personal transformation and the training programmes run
by independent initiatives such as The Clink charity and the
Timpson Foundation, which equip people with skills on the inside and a pathway to a job on the outside. None of this is a
foolproof way to rehabilitate offenders, because there are many
factors at work in the life of a recidivist. But they are examples
of how the exercise of merciful justice can be a means to the
end of restoring an offender, reducing reoffending and making
society a safer place. We need more prisons to be greenhouses
to restore the redeemable.

Some fear that this approach holds too high a view of offenders who, they believe, have forfeited their right to be treated
humanely because of their crimes. A victim of a terrible assault
understandably would feel this, especially if at the trial the per-
petrator expresses little or no remorse. The offended are entitled to feel rage when their life has been violated and the public
has a right to be outraged when those guilty of murder or rape,
especially young offenders, not only show no remorse but also

openly ridicule the court. The anger that this provokes is not only understandable but is also, I would argue, virtuous. Anger is the appropriate, proportionate and just response to an assault on innocence.

From the inner recesses of our conscience, anger is the soul's proper protest at evil. That is one of the reasons why the tabloid press and social media are so hostile to those who wish to see prison do more than just punish the prisoner. People like me, who want to see prison reform, are often dismissive of the popular media and the politicians who court their support. But before dismissing them, we need to acknowledge that they tap into a moral vein which is not just about vengeance but also recognizes that the moral order has been violated when innocence has been destroyed. Instead of ignoring or denying this, reformers would do better to acknowledge it, and then propose how society can reduce the risk of the offender repeating the offence. Although there is virtue in giving vent to the necessary 'no' in response to the violation of a person and his or her property, both the victim and society have to find a way through the maze of anger so that other emotions can play their part in shaping a safer and more constructive future.

I once made a series of programmes for Radio 4 called *The Bishop and the Prisoner*. In one episode, I met a woman who had been raped and nearly murdered. She had consciously decided that her life would not be defined by this traumatic violation. She made the decision to forgive the violent rapist. She used a phrase that has stayed with me. She said, 'forgiveness is fluid'. There were days when it was very hard to remember and to forgive. There were others when forgiveness seemed to flow. It was impossible to predict which days would fall when. The fluidity of forgiveness waxed and waned.

But it is forgiveness that can begin to assuage the anger, not in a neat and decisive break that denies the past, but in a crashing of gears as we move forwards in stops and starts. There is a power in even the most tentative forgiveness that can begin to heal the offended and redeem the offender, perhaps not in every case, but in some. Bringing the offender face to face with the offended is the essence of restorative justice. We need to give it more of a place within the criminal justice system. Understandably, not every person whose life has been violated by another welcomes this opportunity, nor should people be pressurized into engaging with someone who has grievously wounded them. But when it can happen, it begins to humanize the judicial process and turns the system of justice from an impersonal instrument of the State into a personal transaction between the guilty and the innocent. Such personal encounters between the offended and the offender, especially while the latter are in prison, have the capacity to begin to restore the prisoner while at the same time empowering the offended, helping them to manage their trauma and develop their identity, as one woman put it to me, 'from being a victim to becoming the victor'.

Constitutionally, the authority of our judicial system flows from the Crown. Judges are appointed by the sovereign, upon whom authority is conferred in the coronation service. It is rich in signs and symbols, in ritual and in rubric that explains their significance. When the Rod is given to the sovereign, these words are spoken aloud:

Receive the Rod of Equity and Mercy
Be so merciful that you be not too remiss
So execute justice that you forget not mercy
Punish the wicked
Protect and cherish the just.

Justice tempered by mercy. Merciful justice. Such justice is exemplified by a judge of whom it was said that, when he was sentencing, it was as if he were a parent dealing with his own child. When this was put to him he replied, 'You see, we can never forget we are all sinners.'

In his book *The Safest Shield* (Hart Publishing, 2015), a previous Lord Chief Justice, Lord Igor Judge, confessed that you cannot teach 'the essential judicial qualities', which he listed as patience, determination and courage. Then he added, 'and humility – yes, humility – do what you believe to be right'. Lord Judge continued, 'You are entrusted with enormous power over your fellow human beings. People's lives will be in your hands. The exercise of such power over others calls for humility.' As Jane Austen encouraged us, we would all do well to pray, 'Incline us, oh God, to think humbly of ourselves.'

As we have seen, at the beginning and at the end of his public life, Jesus included prisoners within the scope of his mission. In Luke 4.18, he quotes the Old Testament (Isaiah 61.1):

The Spirit of the Lord is upon me,
because he has anointed me . . .
to proclaim release to the captives

Although the Gospels do not record any instance of Jesus freeing anyone from prison, they abound with stories of Jesus liberating men, women and children from the prisons of disease, death, demons and guilt. Towards the end of his own life, as he faced betrayal and imprisonment, Jesus gazed beyond the grave to the world beyond, a world in which the truth of our earthly lives becomes crystal clear. It's a world full of surprise where what has been hidden or kept discreet in this life is exposed to the searching light and sight of God. One of the six tests of how well we have lived our life will be whether or not we have taken care of the prisoner. Those who have and those who have not are equally surprised by the revelation that it is in the prisoner as well as in the hungry, the thirsty, the stranger, the poor and the sick that we have come face to face with Jesus, the Son of Man and Child of the Earth. Jesus was a prisoner, a victim of injustice. To touch the life of any prisoner and, in turn, to be touched by him or her is to connect with the fate and the faith of Jesus himself: 'just as you did it to one of the least of these who are members of my family, you did it to me'. Then, more disturbingly, 'just as you did not do it to one of the least of these, you did not do it to me' (Matthew 25.40, 45).

Postscript

'Thought for the Day', 2 September 2008, when the *Today* programme was broadcast live from Liverpool Prison

In my time, I've been in about ten prisons. Getting in is always the same – the forbidding high wall, the secure doors, the passport for ID, the handing over of your mobile phone – these symbols of freedom surrendered. Very few of us get to go inside a prison, yet most of us have an opinion about who should be there. Over the last ten years, I've been to this prison a number of times. It's the first place I've ever been given a round of applause at the end of a sermon! I like coming and I like meeting prisoners. I confess that something happens to me as I come from the outside to the inside. On the other side of the walls, whenever I hear of yet another crime I feel all the anger that should rise up in us all for yet another innocent victim. But once on the inside and face to face with a prisoner in his cell, the mood can change as you shake the hand of flesh and blood. There's no denying the severity, or even the barbarity, of the prisoner's crime, but often, beneath the banter, there's this pang of loneliness, this flicker of honesty, this sigh of sorrow that calls out from behind the eyes. Of course, some may dismiss this as romantic and sentimental, but I remember on my first visit here, one burly tattooed prisoner butting his head close to mine and in a low voice saying, 'Father, don't think there are any men here who don't cry in their cells at night.' Prison chaplains will tell you that they have many conversations with prisoners about God. They echo the poem 'The prisoner' by R. S. Thomas:

We ransack the heavens,
The distance between
Stars; the last place we look
Is in prison, his hide out
In flesh and bone.

The fundamental question facing our society is whether we see prisons as warehouses to store the incorrigible or greenhouses to restore the redeemable. The way we answer that question will determine the sorts of prisons we build. Especially today, when we hear that charities such as NACRO and Turning Point are joining the list of those bidding to run new prisons.

In his famous parable, of the prodigal son Jesus tells of the father begging the reluctant elder brother to come in to the party to celebrate the return of his penitent younger brother. Jesus told this story to shame self-righteous people who were outraged by the low lifes that he was gathering into God's kingdom. The sight of the father pleading with the elder son to accept the repentance and redemption of his errant brother is a parable for our times.

Although there's clearly a small number of criminals who are never safe to release back into the community, the challenge for us is to create prisons that believe in the possibility of redemption for the 80,000 people in our prisons today.

9

Mercy

After publishing the Hillsborough Independent Panel's report in 2012, I was invited by a group of senior civil servants in the Home Office to take part in a seminar addressing the subject of speaking truth to power. Although the Panel had been set up by the Government and was independent, we often found ourselves under pressure from powerful forces and vulnerable to the threat of judicial review. At the seminar, I shared a platform with Sir Robert Francis QC, who had chaired the inquiry into the negligent care at Stafford Hospital. In the course of the discussion, Sir Robert made an important point about investigations into professional practice, drawing a distinction between errors of judgement and criminal acts. It is a vital differentiation. Few of us have never made an error of judgement. It is something that most of us have to live with, and with contrition.

In spite of the phrase having entered the dictionary of political clichés, we do have to learn lessons from the past. Building on this scrutiny, we have to improve our practices and refine our institutions, but this is different from wilful criminal misconduct, which needs to be addressed separately. Intentional harm, criminal negligence, manslaughter, perverting the course of justice, covering up and shifting the blame to others all require robust criminal investigation. Yet, whether it is errors of judgement, criminal acts or simply our failure to live up to standards according to which we judge other people, there is no one who does not know, to one degree or another, the need for mercy.

For all our longing to live in a fairer world, the sober truth is that a totally just society would be an uncomfortable place for us sinners to find ourselves! 'Sinner' may be an old-fashioned word, but it conveys what we all know, that there is a gap in all of us between what we are and what we ought to be, a chasm between what we expect of others and how we ourselves behave, a ravine between the ideal 'me' of my imagination and the real me of my deeds, words and thoughts. In our call for justice in the world, we can easily overlook the myriad injustices that we ourselves have perpetrated or been complicit in throughout our own lives.

Jesus never sought justice for himself. Even though he was subject to lies, hostile questioning, manipulating malice and murderous plots, his focus was always on seeking justice for others. He was also quite explicit about steering us away from being judgemental: 'Do not judge, and you will not be judged; do not condemn, and you will not be condemned' (Luke 6.37). In other words, from the moment we pass judgement on someone else, we are immediately weighed on the same scales – and found wanting.

Some people don't like the idea of God judging, yet you'll often hear them wondering, 'Why doesn't God do something about the state of the world?' Unpacked, this is, in fact, a call for God to judge the world, to separate out the bad from the good and to remove from the face of the earth all traces and causes of human sadness. Before anyone has a chance to answer such a question, another comes rushing in: 'Who do we think would still be standing?' If God were to uproot every weed and tare, what sort of field would be left? It exposes one of our greatest needs as human beings – the need for mercy!

So many of the encounters Jesus had were with people who, knowingly or unknowingly, were in need of mercy. One was an adulteress. Caught in the act, she was dragged before Jesus so that he would condemn her. There is no mention of the man involved, and all her accusers were men. They weren't really interested in her, they wanted to trip Jesus up and to trap, but he met them with silence. Jesus responded to their haranguing of the woman by quietly writing in the dust on the ground. Eventually, applying the principle of scrutinizing our own lives according to the same standard by which we judge others, Jesus broke the silence: 'Let anyone among you who is without sin be the first to throw a stone at her' (John 8.7).

He knew how devastating such a challenge was. He didn't need to look around for a reaction, so turned his attention back to the ground, as if to say, 'Dust you are and to the dust you shall all return.' The oldest left first. Having lived longer lives, they knew their own misdemeanours and how none of them was faultless. The younger ones with less experience of life were the idealists and ready to pulverize the adulteress, but even youth eventually crept away in shame. Left alone with the woman, Jesus pointed out the retreat of her merciless accusers and added 'Neither do I condemn you' (John 8.11). In the presence of Jesus, she met mercy before judgement and, instead of forensic examination, she found forgiveness. Not that Jesus condoned her adultery: 'From now on do not sin again', he concluded. In and through Jesus, she experienced the compassion of God before being reminded of God's commandment. As Zacchaeus did, she experienced mercy before judgement. Jesus was a pastor showing God's love before he was a prophet pointing out God's law. This primacy of love, mercy, compassion and forgiveness was the foundation of his life. It was as if these virtues had been banked up in eternity, waiting for him to come and unleash them into an unforgiving world.

Very early in my years as a curate, I discovered the extraordinary power of the ministry of mercy. When you are ordained to be a priest by a bishop, you are given authority by God to absolve those who are sorry for their sins. In the words of the Book of Common Prayer, 'Whose sins thou dost forgive, they are forgiven'. This dispensation of mercy is an exceptional gift, both for the recipient and for the minister.

One day, I took a call from a stranger to tell me that a parishioner, unknown to me, was in a local hospital run by nuns, critically ill and likely to die. She asked if I would visit her elderly aunt. I duly did. We had a pleasant conversation at the end of which I asked her if she would like me to say a prayer with her. 'No. Not if you've come to tell me that I'm going to die,' she replied. I asked her if she would like me to come again. She said that she would and I visited her several times. At the end of one of our times together, she voiced the following thought: 'What would God want with a sinner like me anyway?' I tried to say, in as sensitive a way as possible, that it was precisely for sinners that God had sent Jesus into the world, to bathe the wounded with mercy and to make them whole. She was silent. I said a prayer with her permission. The next time I visited, she was asleep. I stayed, prayed silently and left. As I was walking down the corridor, the Sister called out and ran after me: 'Oh Father, she's in great distress. She calls out in the night, "Release me, release me!" ' I turned around and went back into the lady's room and knelt by her bed. Taking her hand, I whispered into her ear softly, 'God loves you. He forgives you. You are forgiven. He releases you. Go in peace.' A few hours later, the phone rang at home. 'Oh, thank you,' cried the Sister, 'she has just died.' Shakespeare called mercy 'the gentle rain from heaven'.

A constant theme throughout all the psalms is the mercy of God. For example, 'O give thanks unto the Lord for he is gracious; and his mercy endures for ever' (Psalm 136.1, 26, adapted from the Book of Common Prayer). Every one of the twenty-seven verses of this psalm ends with the line, 'His mercy endures for ever.' Whatever we do, whatever we throw at God through doubt, disbelief and disobedience, his mercy endures for ever. The Psalms trumpet the triumph of mercy over judgement. I've met those who have said that they would like to believe in God and even to be able to pray, but honestly feel that they're not good enough. What they fail to realize is that this is one of the first signs of faith. The realization of what we're truly like becomes the window through which we begin to see how God reaches out to us, not in judgement, but with mercy. It's as if there's a torrent of mercy rushing from heaven to earth, bursting its banks with compassion. Certainly, none of us is good enough to stand before a perfectly just God. Equally, none of us is so bad that we fall beyond the pale of God's mercy. Ever since I was at school and in the chapel choir, I've held on to those words at the end of the 'Te Deum', which I particularly associate with Stanford's setting: 'O Lord, in Thee have I trusted, let me never be confounded.'

John Buchan, famously the author of *The Thirty-Nine Steps*, wrote another book, called *Sick Heart River*. It is an autobiographical novel about a man confronting his own terminal illness out in the wilds of northern Canada. It contains the line, 'Now there suddenly broke in on him like a sunrise a sense of God's mercy – deeper than the fore-ordination of things, like a great mercifulness'. Buchan observes that, in spite of nature being 'red in tooth and claw', the whole of creation is bathed in divine mercy. He then lists a litany of mercies, which begins:

... but out of the cruel North most of the birds had flown south from ancient instinct, and would return to keep the wheel of life moving. Merciful! But some remained, snatching safety by cunning ways from the winter of death. Merciful! Under the fetters of ice and snow there were little animals lying snug in holes, and fish under frozen streams, and bears asleep in their lie-ups, and moose stamping out their yards, and caribou rooting for their grey moss. Merciful!

Psalm 136 echoes these sentiments, seeing God's enduring mercy in providence: 'Who gives the food to all flesh'; in protection: 'who remembered us when we were in trouble'; in history: 'gave their land . . . for an heritage unto Israel his servant'; and in nature: 'who laid out the earth above the waters' and 'who hath made great lights' (Psalm 136.25, 23, 21, 6, 7, Book of Common Prayer). Sustaining them throughout is the mercy of God 'that endures for ever'.

The greatest revelation of God's mercy is Jesus himself. His very name says it: 'God saves us.' He saves us from everything that is the opposite of mercy: self-hatred, self-destruction, the merciless self, the judgemental nature of others, fear in all its expressions, both false and real. He saves us from ourselves. He saves us, too, from the unavoidable judging of God, who must, out of love, act against those who have any part in the desecration of creation, in which we are all complicit to various degrees. Judgement and mercy are each other's opposites and both flow from the love of God. Love must act against all that diminishes what God has made and love must act in mercy to thwart evil and rescue both victim and transgressor.

The mystery of the incarnation of Christ is that mercy takes the initiative and becomes the disrupter. It triumphs over judgement.

Shakespeare explained how it works through the famous speech of Portia from *The Merchant of Venice*:

The quality of mercy is not strained
It droppeth as the gentle rain from heaven

Upon the place beneath. It is twice blest:
It blesseth him that gives and him that takes . . .
. . . It is an attribute to God Himself;
And earthly power doth then show likest God's
When mercy seasons justice. Therefore, Jew,
Though justice be thy plea, consider this:
That in the course of justice none of us
Should see salvation. We do pray for mercy
And that same prayer doth teach us all to render
The deeds of mercy.

Mercy triumphs because it is more fertile than judgement and spawns seeds and deeds of mercy. We, who are debtors to mercy, become merciful. This was Jesus' explicit teaching: 'Be merciful, just as your Father is merciful' (Luke 6.36). It is the proof of our repentance. Mercy is our change of heart.

This followed directly on from Jesus saying that, 'the Most High . . . is kind to the ungrateful and wicked' (Luke 6.35). We forgive as we have been forgiven; it's locked into the Lord's Prayer: 'Forgive us our trespasses as we forgive those who trespass against us.' The followers of Jesus become the gathering of the forgiven. There can be no more radical a company than a community of the forgiven forgiving.

In the time of Jesus, religious leaders, mainly the Pharisees, were infamous for being quick to judge others. Rather like the clergy in the medieval Church, they loved money and position but, worse than that, they were sticklers for the rules when it came to imposing them on other people. And even worse, according to Jesus, they were, through their hypocrisy, an obstacle to faith, a stumbling block to others believing in God. Even though their private lives told a different story, publicly they put on a good show and enforced religious rituals and the commandments of God.

Self-righteousness was their outer clothing. Jesus agreed with them that the laws of God were to be obeyed, but then he added a curious line: 'Unless your righteousness exceeds that of the scribes and Pharisees, you will never enter the kingdom of heaven' (Matthew 5.20). What could possibly exceed the self-righteousness of these falsely pious leaders? Perhaps their private lives should match their public utterances? Jesus frequently accused them of double standards. They acted the part, but if you took the lid off their inner life, you would be knocked back by the stench of their hypocrisy. Jesus compared it to the smell of a decaying corpse!

But there's another way of understanding the righteousness that 'exceeds that of the Pharisees'. It is a righteousness that contains the quality of mercy. Mercy was the quality that the Pharisees were missing. As Jesus added, without it 'you will never enter the kingdom of heaven'. I know only too well the gap between what I appear to be, as a bishop, and the innermost 'me'. I know that although in public I uphold the rules and the rituals of the Church and the commandments of God, I am utterly dependent on the mercy of God. If my salvation depended on my inner life matching my public role, I'd be without hope, but it's the mercy of God that saves me. A mercy that exceeds righteousness.

As these truths dawned in and renewed the minds of the first Christians they expressed them vividly:

There is therefore now no condemnation for those who are in Christ Jesus.
(Romans 8.1)

He has rescued us from the power of darkness and transferred us into the kingdom of his beloved Son, in whom we have redemption, the forgiveness of sins.
(Colossians 1.14)

Once . . . you had not received mercy,
But now you have received mercy.
(1 Peter 2.10)

Mercy is the path that takes us from judgement to 'no condemnation' and out of a moral darkness into the light. Not because
we're perfect, but because, as the 'Te Deum' tells us, his mercy
'lightens upon us'. Salvation is the triumph of mercy over judgement, but is everybody forgiven, and are people forgiven against
their will?

God's mercy extends to everyone without exception. Of this
I am sure. The Gospels show that God loves the whole world,
not just the favoured few. His mercy knows no bounds. On the
cross Jesus practised his own preaching by loving and praying
for his enemies and persecutors: 'Father, forgive them' (Luke
23.34). With those words and that prayer, he covered the whole
of humanity with mercy.

In so far as it is possible to compare our relationship to God
with a human friendship, I cannot help but reflect that mercy and
forgiveness need to be received before a broken relationship can be
restored. Imagine you discover that a friend has betrayed you. You
are devastated, but determined not to allow the bond between you
to be broken for ever. You address the betrayal. The friend admits
it. You confess your hurt and offer your forgiveness, but the friend
rejects it and you. Although you remain merciful, the relationship
between you can never be restored until the friend yields to your
forgiveness. Only through acknowledging the wrongdoing and
accepting forgiveness can a friendship be mended. So God has
rained mercy on everyone and forgives all, but it is only through
receiving his forgiveness that we can taste the blessing of a restored relationship. The story that Jesus told about the father with
two sons painted a picture of a heartbroken and endlessly patient
father watching for his errant son to come home.

When the dissolute and destitute child appeared on the horizon, the father was waiting. Overcome with compassion, he raced towards him, hugged and kissed him. His mercy was full of energy. The father wouldn't allow his penitent son to complete his prepared speech. His mercy was impatient. He decked him out for a party with fine clothes and jewellery and killed the fatted calf. His mercy was extravagant. They celebrated the prodigal's return with a prodigious feast. The father's mercy was shot through with joy. But the wealth of all that mercy could only be experienced by the son through his returning. Otherwise it remained for him remote and unrealized in spite of his father's longing.

If human freedom means anything, I believe that we must be able to be free to walk into or away from the light. Responding positively to God's love doesn't have to involve religion and rituals. It can be faint and tentative. Like tasting. It can be as *nervous* as the anonymous woman in the crowd who touched Jesus' clothes in desperation and heard him say, 'your faith has made you well' (Matthew 9.22); it can be as *passive* as the paralysed man who let his friends carry him through the roof to the feet of Jesus and heard him say, 'your sins are forgiven' (Matthew 9.2); it can be as *tearful* as the prostitute who spent her money on perfume for Jesus and through her tears heard him say to her, 'your sins are forgiven' and 'your faith has saved you' (Luke 7.48, 50); it can be as *thankful* as the healed leper who returned to show his gratitude by throwing himself down in front of Jesus and hearing him say, 'your faith has made you well' (Luke 17.19); it can be as *self-critical* as Peter, who begged Jesus to leave him because he was so conscious of his sinfulness, yet heard Jesus quieten his soul with, 'Do not be afraid' (Luke 5.10); it can be as *childlike* as the children resting in the arms of Jesus who heard him say, 'To [children] such as these that the kingdom of God belongs' (Matthew 19.14); and it can be at the eleventh hour and fifty-ninth minute as the thief, dying next to Jesus, who cried out, 'Remember me when you come into your kingdom' and heard the immortal words, 'Truly, I tell you, today you will be with me in Paradise' (Luke 23.42-43). All of these tentative responses, each in its own way, were saying 'yes' to the mercy of God 'that endures for ever'.

There might just be many more people in God's eternal kingdom than different religions would admit. There are many faiths of many races whose believers appeal to God's mercy, approach him with awe and seek to act justly. Their fear of God and their commitment to justice are consonant with all that Jesus stood for. As St Peter confessed, 'God shows no partiality' (Acts 10.34).

There are others for whom religion itself has been an obstacle to faith. They have given up practicing the ritual but have held to the values of justice and mercy. There will be some who respond to God's revelation in creation but who feel more spiritually at home in a woodland or a garden and, like John Buchan, experience in nature the deep mercy of God. Yet, sadly, I believe that it is still possible for someone, ultimately, to walk away from the light of God's love.

There's a telling episode in the autobiography of Kenneth Clark, the author of the celebrated television series *Civilisation*. In his book *The Other Half* (Hamish Hamilton, 1986), he writes about an intense and wonderful religious experience that took place in the Church of San Lorenzo in Florence, when his whole being was 'irradiated by a kind of heavenly joy'. It lasted for several months.

He was quite sure that he had felt 'the finger of God', but 'made no effort to retain it'. 'My life was far from blameless: I would have to reform.' He writes with great honesty, 'I was too deeply embedded in the world to change course.' He seems to have come so close to tasting God's mercy. Who knows how his journey might have continued?

God does not impose his love on us, for if he were to compel us in that way, it would not be love. He does not constrain us against our will. His love is vulnerable to our resistance and rejection, just like all true love is. Because of this, the truth is that, although God has mercy and forgives us all, those who refuse his love cannot be forced to taste its blessings. If that love abides for eternity, then so does freedom, for without it there is no love.

So what is the destiny of those who, for whatever reason, willfully turn their face against the gaze of God's grace? If we believe that God is the author of all that is just, then we must trust that our destiny will always unfold justly in his hands. Furthermore, we never know what peace any of us will make with ourselves, and with God, in the closing moments of our life. According to the New Testament, on the horizon beyond the grave stand two realities: heaven and hell. Piecing together the fragments of a mosaic scattered through Scripture, the vision of heaven is that of the human family delighting with God in a renewed creation; the vision of hell is that of a wasteland. In the last book of the Bible, the Revelation of St John, the images of both are kaleidoscopic and colourful.

They bring to a climax a theme that runs through both the Old and New Testaments and through many sacred texts. There is a choice to be made between good and evil, justice and injustice, love and hatred, life and death. We often make wrong choices and are chastened by the consequences through reaping what we sow, but there is always hope, because God's 'mercy endures for ever'. The ultimate choice for free human beings is whether or not we choose mercy.

Divine love chooses not to force us to our knees. Love's nature surrenders to the nails of the cross in the hope that the wounds of the lover will convert the soul of the sinner. The last nail in God's love is the choice of some, freely taken, to put themselves beyond the reach of his enduring mercy.

There is a contemporary postscript to these thoughts on justice and mercy. As a society, we seem to have become strangers to mercy. Mainstream and social media have cultivated a censorious voice and generated a noise devoid of the quality of mercy. People are hunted, hounded, harangued, denounced and destroyed by strident and merciless voices. The public square, instead of being a space to air and debate great ideas, has become a place cordoned off by prejudice. Universities seem to have surrendered the campus to those who have forgotten that these are the places where we are to learn to outwit rather than outlaw those with whom we disagree. This narrowing and cancelling culture seems an increasingly foreign land lacking magnanimity and mercy.

I am sometimes asked if the Hillsborough families should forgive those responsible for 'the unlawful killing' of their 96 loved ones, especially after such a long time has passed. Just as there are stages to grieving, such as denial and depression, so varying emotions follow on from each other when you have been violated. Anger is one of those, and it is a proper and proportionate response to being so deeply hurt. No human being other than the one who is suffering has the right to prescribe when anger should give way to another emotion, just as no one has the right to presume closure for another who is bereaved. Given the inordinate length of time it has taken for the families to pursue the cause and course of justice (thirty-two years as I write) and given the consequent arresting of their grieving, I should imagine that it will take as many decades for them even to contemplate a different response to the loss of their loved ones.

In case anyone should think I am suggesting that the absence of mercy is a secular phenomenon, let me admit that, tragically, in our common history, Jews, Christians and

Muslims have betrayed this quality of mercy. This is the core of our three faiths. In spite of the fact that all three religions are united by a belief in the mercy of God, each of us has been guilty of merciless acts. We are all the more culpable because we confess to a belief in the God of mercy. Jews, when they read their Scriptures, learn about the compassion of God. In Hebrew, the word for 'compassion' comes from the word for 'womb'. The mercy of God is like the love of a mother for her own child and offspring.

Christians hear the mercy of God broadcast to the world from a cross through the voice of the crucified Christ praying for his tormentors to be forgiven. Muslims pray prostrate to God, 'The Merciful One'. But in spite of such confessions of faith, we have frequently acted against our convictions through a history of mercilessness towards one another. These tensions are, tragically, not just historic but also contemporary. It would be a blessing to the world if the three faiths were able to come together in a concordat of mercy, pleading for mercy for our merciless acts in the past, pledging to be merciful to one another now, and promising to measure all our attitudes and actions by the quality of mercy. Such a coming together would not contradict or compromise the convictions of each religion, but would express the faith that we have in common in the mercy of God and in the God of mercy. It is urgent that we no longer be strangers to mercy. The future stability of the world depends on it.

The human heart is marbled with the instinct for fairness. Layered alongside it lies the instinct for freedom. Just as justice and mercy flow from love, so does the instinct to be free, for there can be no coercion to love. That is a truth all lovers know. You can love people with all your heart, but you cannot force them to love you in return. That point is poignantly made in the story of *Beauty and the Beast*. When the Beast decides to let the beautiful Belle go and to risk his own future, his minions scream out in protest, 'Why?' 'I had to let her go because I love her' was his answer.

The same truth is to be found in the Garden of Eden when God loved Adam and Eve into existence. He did not force them either to do good or to love him in return. They were free, as we are free to love whomsoever and whatsoever we choose. That is the liberty love bestows. Every choice has a consequence, as human history never fails to show. Yet that same history also reminds us, the instinct to be free to shape our own destiny is in our DNA. It is a hopeful sign for our future that, in the past, people have always ultimately refused to accept the tyranny of dictators and have risen up to challenge the fascism of autocrats when they have tried to suffocate the human spirit. It may have taken decades, or even centuries, and cost much blood, but the thirst for liberty is unquenchable except by freedom itself and, in the end, it defies oppression.

That aspiration to be free goes hand in hand with the ambition to live in a world that is fair, and certainly fairer than the one exposed by the latest crisis in health and wealth. Fairness, Forgiveness and Freedom. These are the children of Love, Justice, Mercy and Liberty. A trinity of virtues on which to build the new world that is coming.

Postscript

'Thought for the Day', 3 November 2003

Spare a thought for those passengers stranded in the Mediterranean on the cruise ship, the *Aurora*, afflicted by a virus and finally admitted to the Port of Gibraltar. It's triggered in my mind a story I often tell.

Imagine, one day, a rich friend invites you to come on a cruise of a lifetime – all expenses paid! You get to the Pier Head here in

Liverpool and board a luxury liner. You're shown to your suite on A Deck and within hours you're sailing in the sun.

After six weeks of having the time of your life, the question pops into your head as to where you might be going, but you don't wish to appear ungrateful and you carry on enjoying yourself.

After a further six months of high living, you can suppress the question no longer and ask your host where and when this amazing trip might be coming to an end. 'Is there a problem?' he asks, 'Something not to your liking?' 'No,' you reply, 'it's all wonderful!' 'Then eat, drink and be merry,' he says. So you do your best.

After ten years of sailing around, this dream cruise has become a nightmare! 'Please!' you beg your host, 'Just tell me. Where? When?'

Is this ridiculous? No! Here we are on this planet Earth, like a ship cruising through space, and every one of the passengers asks at least once on the journey about where and when it might all come to an end.

Well, imagine, then, recovering your composure, you ask another question: 'How many on this cruise?' He tells you there are a thousand passengers!

'A thousand people?' You can't believe it! 'It feels like only 200!' you protest.

'Oh, yes' he says, 'I thought you'd say that! Because here on A Deck there are only 200. But for the last ten years in the hold of this ship there've been 800 – and they've been on bread and water.' Ridiculous? No! For here on this ship called planet Earth – cruising through space – 20 per cent of us are on A Deck and 80 per cent are in the hold of the ship. And the water they're drinking often isn't pure. This parable prompts many reflections – not least, how on earth, and how on this Earth, can we build staircases between the decks of inequality that are such an offence to God? After yesterday's ordination of the Bishop of New Hampshire, some commentators are saying – and even welcoming – that it spells the end of the Anglican Communion. If that proved to be so, it would be the greatest pity. The Communion is a unique international partnership in which the 80 per cent actually get to meet the 20 per cent on an equal footing.

It's a staircase between the decks, and one of the few international alliances *not* based on either economics or trade, and where unity across cultures brings deeper understanding of the human condition.

Without such relationships, those of us on A Deck can retire to our luxury cabins, less likely to be disturbed by the noise of death below decks and deaf to the cries of injustice that God alone can hear.